THEN AND THERE SERIES

GENERAL EDITOR
MARJORIE REEVES, M.A., PH.D.

Lenin and the Russian Revolution

DONALD W. MACK

Illustrated from contemporary sources

GW00691959

LONGMAN

WD
12/16
KHS

LONGMAN GROUP LIMITED
London

*Associated companies, branches and representatives
throughout the world*

© Longman Group Ltd 1970

y47·0&4

First published 1970
Eighth impression 1978

ISBN 0 582 20457 7

*Printed in Hong Kong by
Sheck Wah Tong Printing Press Ltd*

Contents

To the Reader   iv

1 THE ROMANOVS IN 1914   1

2 RUSSIA IN 1914   7

3 RUSSIA IN THE FIRST WORLD WAR   19

4 THE FEBRUARY REVOLUTION   29

5 LENIN IN EXILE   35

6 TO THE FINLAND STATION   41

7 THE JULY DAYS AND KORNILOV   46

8 SOLDIERS, PEASANTS, WORKERS   54

9 LENIN PERSUADES THE BOLSHEVIKS   60

10 THE BOLSHEVIK REVOLUTION   63

11 PEACE   73

12 CIVIL WAR   79

13 WAR COMMUNISM AND THE N.E.P.   86

14 DEATH OF A HERO   91

   NOTE ON DATES   96

   THINGS TO DO   97

   HOW DO WE KNOW?   98

   FURTHER READING   100

   GLOSSARY   101

To the Reader

About midnight on a hot July night in 1918 a man, his family, their doctor and three servants were abruptly awakened, ordered to dress, and go to the basement of the house in which they were living as prisoners. The man had been, until February 1917, the *Tsar** of Russia, and his wife, Alexandra, the *Tsaritsa*; their children were the Grand Duchesses Olga, Tatiana, Maria and Anastasia, and the Grand Duke Alexis. Now the former Tsar and his family were prisoners of the *Bolsheviks* in a house in Ekaterinburg near the Ural Mountains.

As the Tsar descended the stairs he carried in his arms his sick son Alexis. When they reached the basement the Tsar, Tsaritsa and Alexis were given chairs. The daughters and servants stood. All were quiet. Suddenly a number of men strode into the room. Some were Letts (men from Latvia on the Baltic), two were from the *Cheka,* and the leader was a man from Siberia called Yurovsky. He told Nicholas that a plan to rescue him and his family had been discovered. 'Therefore, Nikolai Alexandrovich, you are all going to be shot.' Nicholas did not seem to understand and said, 'What?' Yurovsky drew his revolver and shot the Tsar. The Letts and the man from the Cheka began firing at the prisoners. The Tsar fell first, then his son Alexis. There were screams and groans from the victims, and the floor was streaming with blood. Then all was quiet, save for a groan from Alexis who was shot again.

The bodies were stripped of their valuables and loaded on to a motor lorry. They were driven to a mine shaft and then

*Words printed in *italics* are explained in the Glossary (p. 101).

The house in Ekaterinburg where the Tsar and his family were murdered

Cellar where the Tsar's family were shot. The marks on the wall show where some of the bullets dislodged plaster

drenched with acid and set on fire—the Bolsheviks wanted to be sure that their enemies could not show the Tsar's bones as holy relics to the peasants.

There had been no trial. The Tsar and his family had been brutally killed as many Russians had been slaughtered by the Tsar's own agents in the past. The Bolsheviks were the rulers of Russia, but were fighting desperately to defeat their enemies within Russia and the foreigners who were helping them. The Tsar's family was killed so that there should not be any member of the family the Bolsheviks' enemies could rally round, so that it would be clear that they would stop at nothing, and so that the Bolsheviks themselves would realise that there was no turning back—they must win or die.

Yet only five years before, at a great ceremony in St Petersburg, Tsar Nicholas II had celebrated the three-hundredth anniversary of his *dynasty*—the first member of his family, the Romanovs, had become Tsar of Russia in 1613. What had brought Nicholas II from the throne in Kazan Cathedral, St Petersburg, to a miserable death in a cellar in Ekaterinburg?

Tsar Nicholas and the Tsaritsa Alexandra in 1913, wearing historical costume to celebrate the 300th anniversary of the Romanoff family on the throne of Russia

1 The Romanovs in 1914

In 1914 Tsar Nicholas II was an *autocrat*. Unlike the rulers of most other European countries, he did not require to consult anyone else before he made a decision affecting his country. Naturally he had advisers, but he was not bound even to listen to their advice, far less to take it. He chose and dismissed his ministers at will. He believed, as did many of his people, that he had been appointed by God and that God supported him in his actions. Now it is of course important that a man with such tremendous power should be strong minded, and should be able to make clear and definite decisions. But this Nicholas was quite unable to do. Indeed, one writer who knew him said that not only was Nicholas incapable of ruling Russia, he was 'unfit to run a village post office'. And Nicholas said of himself, 'Whatever I try, nothing succeeds.' Nicholas seemed almost to have a gift for doing the wrong thing. On the day of his coronation in 1896 over a thousand people were killed in a stampede because the officials had bungled the arrangements. Yet that evening the Tsar and Alexandra went to a ball given by the French Ambassador. People were naturally shocked that the Tsar appeared to show so little feeling over the death of so many of his subjects.

He seemed to those who met him to be gentle and agreeable, but this may have been because he disliked disagreeing with anyone to his face.

Kerensky, for a time Russian Prime Minister in 1917, said of him: 'The daily work of a ruler he found terribly boring. He could not stand listening long or seriously to ministers' reports, or reading them. He liked such ministers as could tell   1 an amusing story and did not weary his attention with too much business.'

The ministers would discuss things with him and he would nod and seem to agree with them. However, he would change his mind again after seeing someone else, so that some ministers despaired of ever getting him to make up his mind at all. One writer has said that 'whoever saw him last made up the Tsar's mind'. Nicholas was not stupid, and had a very good memory; but he tended to be very stubborn at times, and usually about the wrong things.

The Tsar was indecisive. In contrast the Tsaritsa was too strong-willed. Before her marriage she had been princess Alex of Hesse-Darmstadt (in Germany), and she was a granddaughter of Queen Victoria. She fell in love with Nicholas the first time she saw him, when she was fourteen, and determined to marry him. They were very happy together, and had five children. The first four were girls and the fifth was the much longed-for boy. But the Tsar and Tsaritsa were utterly distressed to learn that Alexis, the heir to the throne, suffered from a dreadful disability, *haemophilia,* and for this Alexandra (as she was called in Russia) blamed herself. She resolved to do all in her power to ensure that Alexis survived to inherit the throne from his father, and that he too, like Nicholas, should be an autocrat. Having made up her mind about this, Alexandra proceeded to make up Nicholas's mind too, and Nicholas agreed with her, perhaps because it was too much trouble to disagree—he signed letters to her 'your poor little weak-willed hubby'; and she encouraged Nicholas to be an autocrat. 'They must learn to tremble before you,' she told him.

Alexandra was a deeply religious person. She had had to change to the *Greek Orthodox* religion (the main religion of Russia) when she married 'Nicky' (as she called her husband) but she began to behave very strangely. She hoped that faith might help to cure Alexis of his illness, and wanted to find a holy man who could pray for her and help her son. In 1905, she found one. The Tsar's diary tells us this: 'We have got to

Rasputin surrounded by admiring ladies of the Tsar's Court

know a man of God—Gregory—from the Tobolsk province.'
'Gregory' was better known as Rasputin, a nickname which
stuck. It means roughly 'the ill-behaved one', and was perfect
for Rasputin who was a rowdy thief, often drunk, unwashed
and smelly. He could hardly read or write, but became a
wandering 'holy man' of a kind at one time common in Russia.
He gathered a group of followers, mostly well-off women, and
introduced them to his own particular religious idea which was
roughly that to obtain forgiveness it was necessary to sin a
great deal, and Rasputin, of course, was very good at showing
how to sin. At last he came to the notice of the Tsaritsa and
he proved to be able to help Alexis when he became very ill.
Haemophilia leads to bleeding at the slightest knock or cut,
bleeding which is very difficult to stop. The best doctors in the
world (and the Tsar could afford the best) were unable to help
Alexis, yet Rasputin seemed to be able to do so. How he did
it, no one knows for sure; Rasputin himself said that he used
drugs or 'will-power'. Anyway, he helped the boy on several
occasions and his parents, were, of course, immensely grateful.

Nicholas once said of him: 'He is just a good, religious, simple-minded Russian. When in trouble or assailed by doubts I like to have a talk with him, and always feel at peace with myself afterwards.'

Alexandra was convinced that God had sent Rasputin as the saviour of Alexis, the heir to the throne.

More and more the Tsar and Tsaritsa relied on him. They took his advice on all sorts of questions and especially on who the Tsar's ministers and officials should be. Able men refused to be polite to Rasputin and were dismissed. Inferior men were put in their place, and the government grew worse. Many knew that Rasputin was evil and they despised him. Since the royal family were so friendly with him, they tended to be despised too, and so the Tsar's friendship with Rasputin weakened his hold on the government of Russia. The Russian proverb 'Fish rots from the head down' was being shown to be true.

Russian Empire in 1914

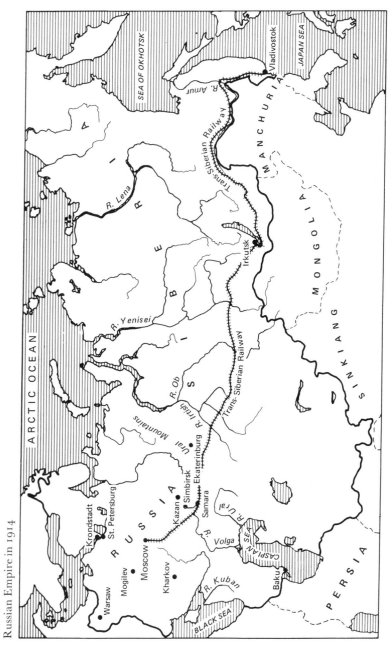

2 Russia in 1914

In 1914 Russia was (as it is now) the largest country in the world. It stretched from the Baltic Sea in the west to the Pacific Ocean in the east, and from the White Sea and Arctic Ocean in the north to the Black Sea in the south.

It was larger than the present-day Soviet Union, including as it did then Finland and most of Poland. Its area was over 7 million square miles. Most of its population of 164 million were Russians, but there were millions of non-Russians also. And, although the population was very large, there were huge areas where there were hardly any people at all—especially in the cold bare parts north of the Arctic Circle.

This vast country was, compared with western Europe, very backward. It had, for its size, few factories; its farms had hardly any machinery and there were few railways (except those leading to the German frontier—which were mainly built to carry soldiers in the event of a war). The great exception was the Trans-Siberian railway which ran from Moscow to Vladivostok on the Pacific. Russian roads were very poor— not unlike those of England in the eighteenth century before the great engineers like Telford and Macadam got to work (see the 'Then and There' book: 'Roads and Canals in the Eighteenth Century'). In much of Russia the rivers were the main way by which people travelled or moved goods about, but most rivers were frozen for several months of the year.

When Tsar Nicholas filled up his *census* form in 1897 he gave as his 'profession' 'Ruler of Russia' and for his *occupation* wrote 'Master of the Russian Earth'. The Tsar was helped in governing the country by his civil servants and ministers. Since he

could dismiss his ministers when he liked, they were naturally careful not to offend him, and though he chose some good men, far more of his ministers were people who were disliked. Naturally the Tsar was considered foolish and unwise for having chosen them.

There was no parliament in Russia to help the government make decisions, but there was the *Duma,* a group of people whom the Tsar had grudgingly agreed to allow to be elected in 1906. This was after a revolution had taken place in 1905. Russia had been beaten by Japan in a war. The Russians had been badly led and armed; the fighting was near Japan and a long way from St Petersburg, and the Japanese were well armed and well trained. They won the main battles—including one at Tsushima where a Russian fleet, which had sailed all the way from the Baltic to the Pacific, was destroyed in a very short time. There were riots and strikes and the crew of the battleship 'Potemkin' mutinied in the Black Sea, murdered some of the officers, and eventually sailed off to Rumania. The Tsar agreed to the Duma because he had been frightened during the revolution. When it had been crushed, however, he regretted giving his consent, and gradually the number of people who could vote for members of the Duma was cut down, till at last, by 1914, most of its members were elected by

landowners. It could do very little, but the Tsar was displeased even at that.

The landowners were the main people involved in governing the country districts too. There *Zemstvos* had been set up to govern but, of course, the Tsar interfered here also. Yet the Zemstvos did manage to do some good work—building hospitals, orphanages, and especially schools. Schools were very necessary because so many Russians were illiterate. More than half the people of Russia could not read or write. Many of those who had had some schooling never read at all once they left school. The Tsar's government did little to help its people—partly because to give everyone an education would cost a lot of money (and the government's spending worked out at 1s 8d a year for each Russian child), partly because some ministers feared that people who could read might read books favouring revolution and the overthrow of the Tsar. Anyway, the Zemstvos worked hard at setting up schools, and at length even the Tsar agreed that every Russian child should go to school—from 1922 onwards!

One of the ways in which the Tsar ensured that his orders were carried out and kept himself informed of what was happening in Russia was through the secret police or *Okhrana*. There were many secret agents—perhaps 20,000 or so—and 9 they kept watch on large numbers of people who were suspected of being likely to cause trouble. But the secret police also watched the members of the government, and they even *intercepted* and read the letters of Nicholas's mother, the former Tsaritsa! There were secret police in schools and clubs, and some were in the Duma, pretending to be members of various groups and speaking on their behalf. Everyone felt nervous that he might be being watched, and afraid that a knock on the door at dead of night meant his arrest, and so the police were very unpopular. No one could trust anyone else. On one occasion a secret policeman, pretending to be a revolutionary, gave warning that one of the Tsar's ministers was to be assassinated. Careful precautions were therefore taken, and the secret policeman was brought in to help. Whereupon he, the member of the Okhrana, shot the minister. He had, in fact, been a revolutionary pretending to be a secret policeman!

When someone was arrested and accused of plotting against the Tsar he might be sentenced to *exile* in Siberia, the enormous area of eastern Russia stretching from the Ural Mountains to the Pacific Ocean. Convicts were often marched on foot, covering the vast journey by slow stages. They were generally in chains, 'the golden bracelets of the Tsar', and their wives and families went too, in wagons. Those who were exiled (the Russians called them 'the unlucky') were often severely treated, and forced to work in new settlements which were being made in Siberia. There they had to endure blazing summer heat and a winter cold worse than that of the North Pole. They were punished for disobedience by a kind of whip called a *knout,* and there was a rule for the guards that if a prisoner died while being flogged the 'remaining strokes were to be inflicted on the corpse'. Leon Trotsky, later one of the Bolshevik leaders, was exiled to Siberia, and described his life there:

'We were going down the River Lena, a few barges of convicts with an escort of soldiers, drifting slowly along with the current. It was cold at night, and the heavy coats with which we covered ourselves were thick with frost in the morning. All along the way, at villages decided on earlier, one or two convicts were put ashore. . . . It took about three weeks till we came to our village which . . . had about a hundred peasant huts. . . . At night the cock-roaches filled the house with their rustlings as they crawled over table and bed, and even over our faces. From time to time we had to move out of the hut for a day or two and keep the door wide open, at a temperature of 35 degrees below zero. Coachmen had to break the icicles off horses' muzzles as they drove along. . . . In the summer our lives were made wretched by midges. They even bit to death a cow that had lost its way in the woods. The peasants wore nets of tarred horsehair over their heads. In the spring and autumn the village was buried in mud.

'Some peasants would help carry the prisoners away secretly in boats, or carts, or on sledges, and pass them along from one to another. The police in Siberia were as helpless as we were. The huge size of the country was both friend and enemy. It was very hard to catch a runaway, but the chances were that we would be drowned in the river or frozen to death in the forest.'

The Tsar's rule was harsh, therefore, and on occasion cruel. Meetings were sometimes broken up by troops: in 1905 a crowd who were trying peacefully to present a petition to the Tsar were fired upon at close range and hundreds were

The Tsar's troops firing on the crowd in front of the Winter Palace in January, 1905

slaughtered. Even 'little boys who had climbed the trees to watch what was going on were shot down like birds'. Troops were often sent also to deal with trouble among the peasants and workers. In retaliation attacks were made on ministers and even on the Tsar himself: once in 1905, during what was supposed to be a twenty-one gun salute to the Tsar, when cannon firing blanks were set off, one turned out to be loaded with a live shell which exploded uncomfortably near the Tsar and his friends! Everything seemed to be done with violence in Russia, and one group of revolutionaries, the Bolsheviks, even obtained some of their party funds by smash-and-grab raids on banks.

Naturally the Tsar's harsh government led people to oppose him, in spite of the difficulties and dangers involved. The workers and peasants were concerned mainly with making enough money to live on and had little energy for revolt. But among the writers, teachers, lawyers and students there were many who were prepared to risk their lives to try to overthrow the government.

One of the Tsar's strongest supports came from the official Russian Church, called the Greek Orthodox Church. He himself was its head and its bearded priests were his loyal servants and were encouraged to try to force people with other beliefs— Catholics, Muslims etc.—to accept Orthodoxy. This made the Church unpopular and, since the Tsar and the Church were on such good terms, the Tsar, too, suffered unpopularity. The Church had a strong hold on the peasants, mainly because their lives were so miserable that the Church's promise of another life in heaven was attractive.

The Orthodox Church's harsh treatment of people with other faiths was all the more stupid because so many of the people who lived in Russia were neither Orthodox nor Russian. Thirty-five in every hundred Russian citizens were not Russian, they did not speak Russian as their native language and they thought of themselves as Poles or Finns or Georgians or Kalmuks and so on. They were peoples whose lands had been conquered by Russia as that country had steadily grown through the centuries from a small area around Moscow to a vast empire. The Tsar treated these non-Russians worse than the Russians themselves and began attempting what was called *Russification*—trying to make them Russians whether they liked it or not. In Poland, for example, the Polish language was forbidden in the schools and the children had to do all their studies in Russian. The Jews, too, were extremely harshly treated and there were pogroms, attacks on the Jews, from time to time—generally when things were going badly for the Tsar. By encouraging attacks on the Jews he could divert attention from his own failures. It is not surprising that many important revolutionaries—Stalin and Trotsky among them— were from non-Russian families.

Although, compared with Britain, Russia had little industry, there was a great surge of factory building before 1914, and the amounts of coal, iron and steel produced greatly increased. Factories got larger and so the workers were brought together in greater numbers. This made them even more aware of their dreadful conditions. Their hours of work were long—11 to 14 per day—and their wages low, while bread was

Living conditions for two Russian workers at the beginning of the twentieth century

dear. Their factories were unsafe and dirty, their houses often merely rooms in a factory barracks which might have to be shared with a family on another shift. There was little machinery to make work easier—in the mines of the Donbas coal-tubs were handled by men, and at the Baku oil wells men spent ten hours turning a winch (the writer Maxim Gorky gave his account of the oil wells the title 'A Portrait of the Depths of Hell'.) The government made some efforts to improve the conditions of the workers by introducing insurance schemes for workers who fell sick or were injured by machinery, and they allowed the workers to have trade unions. Strikes were forbidden, yet occurred nonetheless. The gold miners of the Lena River in Siberia went on strike in 1912. The government brought up troops who fired on the workers killing 200 of them. A priest called to the hospital to attend the dying described the scene:

'In the first ward I saw wounded workers carelessly dumped on the floor and on the bunks. . . . The air was filled with the moaning of victims. I had to kneel down among huge pools of blood to give the *last rites* and I had hardly time to finish with one man before I was summoned to the next. All the dying men swore that their intentions had been peaceful. . . . I believed them. A dying man does not lie.'

There were over 2,000 strikes in 1913 and the workers hated the Tsar and his government.

Many people, however, thought that the peasants (about three-quarters of the Russian population) had a deep love for their Tsar, whom they called 'Little Father'. The year 1917 showed how wrong this belief was, and indeed the peasants had good reasons for disliking the Tsar. Till 1861 most Russian peasants had been *serfs*. In that year they were freed, but had to pay heavily for their land to their former lords. The peasants were poor and a bad harvest could bring famine (so severe at times that animals had to be fed the thatch from the cottage roofs.) The land was poor in many parts of Russia, except for the famous '*Black Earth*' belt, and the peasants' holdings were divided into scattered strips as

During the famine of 1891–2 the peasants were reduced to stripping thatch from their houses to feed their livestock

Peasant women in Kirghizia before the First World War

in parts of England in the early eighteenth century (see the 'Then and There' book, 'The Agrarian Revolution'). It was difficult for them to make enough money to get a decent house, so they often lived in wood or turf huts with earthen floors and little furniture. The animals shared the huts with the humans. Before 1914 the government decided to help some peasants by allowing strips to be blocked together in groups, and some peasants were encouraged to migrate to Siberia, leaving more land for the rest. Others formed *co-operatives* and helped each other. But the changes only made the wealthier peasants, *kulaks,* even better off and though they were naturally pleased by the Tsar's actions, the poor peasants were angry, especially when they had to borrow tools and seed corn from the kulaks and repay it with heavy interest.

An Englishman wrote an account of a Russian village near St Petersburg in 1914:

'The village consists of one street, containing about thirty-five cottages, and lined with birch trees. Behind the village stretch open fields with a long line of forest in the background. The broad, swiftly flowing river is a highway in the summer. . . . Barges are towed up early in the season and come down later with timber cut small or with immense stacks of hay. There are plenty of fish and the peasants cast their nets and catch enough for food and for sale.

'But in November the river freezes hard and remains frozen till April. Then all the steamers and boats and barges lie still, and the river becomes simply a smooth white road over which sleighs go sliding in a long and silent procession.

'The cottages are built of wood and are unpainted. . . . The entrance is from the side. You mount a wooden staircase or ladder, push open a door, and find yourself in the upper or main floor of the cottage, the ground floor being used mainly for storage purposes. A big, white-washed brick stove is in the main room, and on this stove the older people and children sleep in the winter. There is a rough table and a few chairs, a bed and in the middle of the room a child's cot suspended from the ceiling.

'At the end of the village is a bath house, containing a large brick stove on which cold water is poured to produce steam. The bath is a combination of perspiring and washing in hot and cold water, and the peasants help by beating themselves with birch twigs. In winter the youths sometimes rush out of the bath house and roll naked in the snow.

'The main food is home-made rye-bread. The peasant eats meat rarely, as a rule only on feast days. But every day there is a soup of some kind. Barley and porridge are eaten. To drink there is plain water and tea. Every peasant cottage has its *samovar* or tea-urn, and tea is drunk regularly, very weak and very pale, without milk. In drinking tea a small lump of sugar is made to go a long way; a tiny morsel is bitten off and held between the teeth and gradually melts as the tea is sipped.

'The women make their own and the children's clothing, and also the men's shirts or blouses. In the autumn a tailor goes from cottage to cottage and makes rough suits and overcoats for the men. There is a felt-maker too who beats out the felt for the winter boots. The women dress in cotton skirts and blouses and on their heads wear coloured cotton kerchiefs. The men's trousers are tucked into high boots.'

The peasants were very important to the Tsar. Much of the grain they produced was exported, and the money obtained was used to buy locomotives, machines, and equipment for the Russian armies. The peasants, too, provided the soldiers of the Tsar and in 1914 they were the people on whom the Tsar was going to depend.

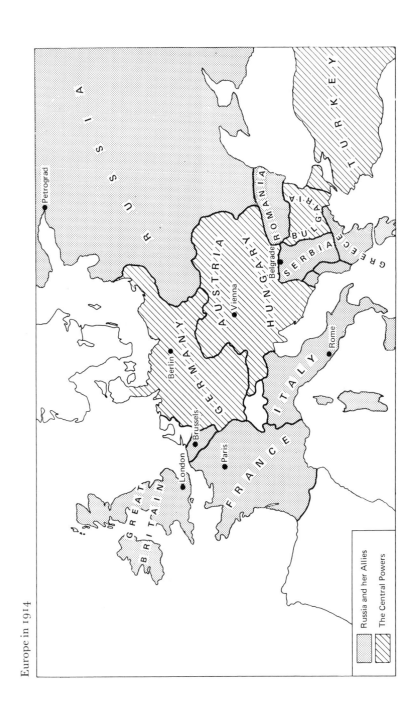

Europe in 1914

Petrograd

RUSSIA

TURKEY

ROMANIA

BULGARIA

GREECE

SERBIA

Belgrade

AUSTRIA

HUNGARY

Vienna

GERMANY

Berlin

Brussels

ITALY

Rome

London

Paris

FRANCE

GREAT BRITAIN

Russia and her Allies

The Central Powers

3 Russia in the First World War

In June 1914 the Austrian *Archduke* Franz Ferdinand was visiting the town of Sarajevo, then part of the Empire of Austria-Hungary, a huge country which was divided up at the end of the First World War. A young *Serbian* called Princip *assassinated* the Archduke as a protest against the fact that many Serbs were ruled by Austria. The Austrian government decided that the time had come for it to go to war with Serbia (a small country which is now part of Yugo-Slavia) and crush it. Now Serbia was an ally of Russia, and the Russians decided to help the Serbs, while Germany decided to help its ally Austria. This meant that France, for twenty years Russia's ally, had to join in too. And when Germany invaded France through Belgium, which Britain had promised to protect, Britain joined France and Russia. So began the First World War (1914–18). Other countries entered the war later, but the main battles were fought on the *Western Front* (mainly the French and British against the Germans), and the *Eastern Front* (mainly the Russians against the Germans and Austrians).

When war was declared some Russians were joyful. A solemn religious ceremony was held in St Petersburg. (The city's name was changed to Petrograd, its Russian form; St Petersburg was the German form given by the Tsar Peter the Great who had founded the city 200 years before.) The Tsar held aloft a Bible and said: 'Officers of my Guard here present, I salute in you the whole army. I bless it. Solemnly I swear that I shall not make peace so long as a single enemy soldier remains on the soil of the fatherland.' The crowd sang 'God save the Tsar'. A writer, Paustovsky, said of this time: 19

'Russia herself was on the move, in thousands of villages throughout the length and breadth of the country, church bells rang the alarm, announcing the *mobilisation*. Thousands of ill-fed peasants' horses trundled the *conscripts* to the stations. . . . The whole country was an armed camp. Everything was in confusion.'

In the Duma most of the members offered their support to the Tsar, as did people from most of the various national groups in Russia. The workers were not too keen on the war, but they held many fewer strikes in the latter half of 1914. The peasants regarded war as a misfortune which would have to be endured like plague or famine.

The Russian army was stronger in 1914 than it had ever been, but so was the German. And the Russians had far fewer of the weapons which were going to be so important: heavy artillery and machine-guns. They had much less ammunition in reserve also, and fewer factories for making more. The main strength of the Russian army was in its *infantry*, largely composed of peasants, who proved to be brave and stubborn fighters. The Russian army was so large in 1914 ($3\frac{1}{2}$ million men were called up for battle in that year) that her allies talked of the 'Russian steamroller' which could crush the Germans. But, in fact, many of the Russian soldiers had not even rifles and had to pick up guns from the dead or wounded. And the Russian methods of supplying their soldiers were faulty, so that shells and food did not reach the men who needed them. Supplies sent by Britain and France piled up at the ports because there were not enough trains to carry them to the front. Even the trains were worn out and could not be replaced. There was no proper method of caring for the wounded who suffered dreadfully as a result. The head of the Duma went to find out about the wounded when reports of bad treatment came back. He wrote:

'*Freight* trains came into Moscow, in which the wounded lay without straw, often without clothing, badly bandaged, unfed for several days. . . . These trains were standing at stations yet volunteer nurses were not allowed on to

Tsar Nicholas, 'the little father' holding an icon, blesses his troops in 1915

Supplies being hauled up to the Front by Russian soldiers in the First World War

them. . . . The army had neither wagons nor horses, nor first aid supplies. . . . We visited the Warsaw station where there were about 17,000 men wounded in battles. At the station we found a terrible scene: on the platforms in dirt, filth and cold, in the rain, on the ground, even without straw, wounded who filled the air with heart-rending cries, dolefully asked: "For God's sake order them to dress our wounds, for five days we have not been attended to." It must be said that after the bloody battles these wounded had been hauled in complete disorder in freight cars and abandoned at the station without aid. The only medical people who attended these unfortunates were Warsaw doctors aided by volunteer nurses. . . .'

Paustovsky worked for a time on a hospital train. He described his life after one battle:

'More and more wounded came. . . . They all seemed to have the same greenish-white, unshaven face, the same eyes, round and white with pain, the same rapid helpless breathing, and the same steel fingers which they dug into us as we held on to them. Our arms were pinched black and blue.

'Only once did I get out for a few minutes at some Polish station to have a smoke. It was evening. The rain had just stopped. Puddles glittered on the platform. A storm cloud like an enormous bunch of grapes hung in the greenish sky, barely touched by the faint pink afterglow.

'Women and children were milling round the train. The women were drying their eyes on their shawls. "Why are they crying", I wondered, until I became aware of the low moaning which came from the coaches.

'Our whole train was ceaselessly, wearily moaning. No mother could hold out against this cry for help and pity without bursting into tears.'

The Russian commanders made many mistakes. The commander-in-Chief at the start of the war was the Grand-Duke Nicholas, the Tsar's uncle. He was astonished to be appointed and wept because he did not know what he was supposed to do. Planning was difficult because, as the Tsar explained to his wife: 'Often we make mistakes because the maps we have were made eighteen years ago and since then some of the forests have disappeared while new woods and villages have appeared.'

The Russian soldiers had been trained according to the teachings of a general who had died long before machine-guns were invented. And the Tsar's minister in charge of the war boasted that he had read no book on army affairs for twenty-five years!

Part of the trouble was that the Russians were always loyal to their allies, Britain and France. Any time these two got into difficulties they asked the Russians to mount a great attack, to force the Germans to move troops from the Western to the Eastern Front. And the Russians always tried to help, suffering terrible losses in the process. 'I wish we did not ask them to do too much', said the British *Ambassador* in Petrograd, but the Russians did too much, so that by the end of the war, out of the 15 million men who were called to serve in the army, nearly 9 million were killed, wounded or taken prisoner.

The Russians had planned to attack the Austrians in 1914 but the French were in terrible danger and asked the Russians to attack the Germans. The Russians did so, German troops were moved to the east, and Paris was saved. But the Russians

Russian dead in quickly dug graves beneath simple wooden crosses

suffered two crushing defeats in eastern Germany. Foolishly the Russian commanders sent wireless messages without putting them into a secret *code*; thus the Germans knew exactly what the Russians plans were. The Russians found that they could fight well against the Austrians, but by 1915 Germany was helping her Austrian ally. Thus the Russians suffered further defeats, and the story of 1916 was the same. The battlefields were fearful. Often whole Russian regiments were wiped out by German guns. During one Russian attack in Poland in 1916 many of the Russian wounded drowned in the mud which was produced by a sudden thaw. The Russian guns could not be brought through the mud and the soldiers got no hot food. Then an icy wind brought a severe frost and men froze to death or suffered from frost-bite. And all the time German shelling had to be endured. In five weeks of such fighting the Russians lost 250,000 men. The soldiers got more and more angry, less and less inclined to fight. Some Russian

German infantry in a trench on the Eastern Front

Barbed wire on the Eastern Front in the First World War

Russian troops fleeing from German cavalry, 1917

prisoners of war who were freed by Cossacks said angrily: 'Who the devil asked you to do that? We don't want to starve and freeze again.' Food and clothing were always short, and many soldiers shot off their own trigger fingers so that they would not have to fight again. Indeed Rasputin warned the Tsar in 1916 that if the fighting went on 'the soldiers will return like wild beasts'.

The Russians who were at home suffered too. Prices of food and clothes rose while wages remained at the old level, so that the people became poorer. Food was short, partly because the peasants could buy little for the money they got, partly because the railways were so busy taking supplies to the front that there were too few trains to bring food from the countryside to the cities. Coal was very short too, so that cold was added to hunger. The peasants remained quiet, but the townworkers began to riot and go on strike. Moreover, peasants and workers alike were annoyed that the sale of vodka was stopped during the war, yet it was well known that the well-to-do got as much as they wanted—served in restaurants from teapots to pretend that the law was being obeyed!

The members of the Duma questioned the Tsar's ministers about the mistakes and shortages, and the Tsar agreed to make some changes in the Government. This angered the

Russian refugees, retreating from the battle areas

Tsaritsa and Rasputin, and they persuaded him to dismiss the Grand-Duke Nicholas (whom Rasputin disliked because, when he had wanted to pay a visit to the front, Nicholas had telegraphed, 'Come and I'll hang you'). The replacement was to be the Tsar himself, who had no military training whatever! Worse still, when the Tsar went off to the front, the head of the government became in effect, the Tsaritsa. As Nicholas wrote to her: 'Think wifey, will you not come to the assistance of your hubby, now that he is absent?' And the Tsaritsa was, of course 'assisted' by Rasputin. No decent man would remain a minister now that Rasputin was helping to run the government, and most of the ministers appointed were scoundrels. Even they did not last for long and there were so many changes that people talked of 'minister's leap-frog'.

The Tsaritsa became more and more hated. People called her 'Nemka', the German woman, and some said that she and Rasputin were helping the Germans. Bruce-Lockhart, a Briton living in Russia at this time, wrote a famous book 'British Agent' about his experiences. He tells of the most popular joke in Moscow:

'Alexis is seen crying in the Winter Palace. A general pats the boy's head,

"What is wrong, my little man?"

Alexis replies:

"When the Russians are beaten, papa cries. When the Germans are beaten mama cries. When am I to cry?"'

(Later, when she was a prisoner, Alexandra said: 'I don't understand why people speak ill of me. I have always loved Russia since I first came here, I have always sympathized with Russia. Why do people think I am siding with Germany and our enemies? There is nothing German about me. I am English by education and English by my language.') What worried people was that the Germans seemed to be able to get news of the Russian plans even before the Russian generals who were to carry them out—and Rasputin knew them too, because the Tsaritsa told him, as, for example, in this letter to the Tsar: 'Our friend says about the new orders you gave to

General Brusilov: "Very satisfied with father's orders, all will be well." He won't mention it to a soul, but I had to ask his blessing for your decision.'

Probably Rasputin did not actually sell secrets to the Germans, but let them slip out when he was drunk—as he often was. Then they would be picked up by the many German spies in Petrograd.

The ministers got worse and worse, but still the Tsaritsa supported Rasputin because as she wrote to the Tsar: 'He lives for you and Russia. And we must give a strong country to baby and dare not be weak for his sake, else he will have a yet harder reign, setting our faults to right.'

People began to complain openly about the war and the mistakes of the government. Officers were afraid to lead attacks in case they should be shot in the back by their own men. Everyone except the Tsar and Alexandra seemed to realise that changes were necessary. Even members of the Tsar's family met secretly to consider whether the Tsaritsa could be got rid of—perhaps by putting her in a nunnery. No one did anything, however, till a young man, Prince Yusupov (who is still alive) and some friends decided that Rasputin must be got rid of. Late in 1916 Yusupov invited Rasputin to his home and fed him on poisoned wine and cakes. Rasputin munched away apparently unaffected, while Yusupov played the guitar, waiting for his guest to die. At last, in desperation, he borrowed a revolver and shot Rasputin, who still did not die, but crawled about bellowing in pain and rage. Yusupov and his friends then seized clubs and beat their victim about the head. Finally they hurled the body through a hole in the ice of the River Neva. The Tsar attended the funeral. The murder of Rasputin had come too late to change anything. Two months later Russia rebelled against her Tsar.

4 The February Revolution

By February 1917 most Russians were thoroughly disgusted by the rule of Tsar Nicholas II, yet when revolution against the Tsar finally came, it seemed to be quite haphazard, and took everyone by surprise. It began over bread, or rather the shortage of it. Indeed one writer said that 'Tsar hunger' began the revolution. In Petrograd long queues of women and boys were told at the end of February that there was no bread. The people refused to believe this, and began to riot. The police tried to stop them, so the people began to fight with them and shout, 'down with the police', and, 'down with the war'. The riots got worse, and the factory workers joined in, many going on strike—especially the 30,000 men from the great Putilov factory. At this point the government called in the army, but

A bread queue in Petrograd, February, 1917

though there were 160,000 troops in Petrograd, they were nearly all recent recruits who had not been properly trained and who did not obey orders unthinkingly. They refused to shoot down the people of Petrograd who were only asking for bread and peace. Then some of the soldiers began to join the workers in their protests against the government. They refused to obey their officers, some of whom were killed, while others fled. And the soldiers began to shoot the police who were still fighting for the Tsar; indeed people believed that the police had machine-guns on rooftops and in church towers from where they could fire on the crowds. Even the *Cossacks* refused to fight for the Tsar, and the government was quite powerless.

The Tsaritsa was convinced that nothing was really wrong. She wrote to her husband: 'This is a hooligan movement, young people run and shout that there is no bread, simply to create excitement, along with workers who prevent others from working. If the weather were very cold they would all probably stay at home. But all this will pass and become calm. . . .'

The Tsar decided, however, to act, and he acted foolishly. He gave orders that the Duma was not to meet. The Petrograd workers and soldiers marched to the palace where the Duma met to show that they supported it. Some members of the Duma decided that they must form a committee to discuss what should be done. Meanwhile, the workers, too, formed a council, the Russian word for which is *Soviet*. By this time the revolutionaries had control of Petrograd; they took over some of the government buildings and the Tsar's officials were no longer obeyed. The Duma's committee sat among heaps of guns, grenades, and boxes of bullets. They decided that the Tsar's government was at an end, and that they must set up a new, temporary one, called the *Provisional* Government. The Tsar set off from his headquarters to go to his palace near Petrograd, but the revolutionaries had many friends among the railway workers who diverted the train to Pskov. The Tsar was utterly bewildered by the collapse of his power and on the 30 next day he *abdicated,* saying that his son should be the new

A patrol, Petrograd, February, 1917

Charging Cossack Cavalry

Tsar. He soon realised that a sick boy could not possibly rule at such a time and so named as head his brother the Grand-Duke Michael. But Michael was persuaded that his life might be in danger, so he agreed that all power should go to the Provisional Government.

The head of the new government was Prince Lvov, but a very important member of it was a young lawyer, Alexander Kerensky, a member of the Duma for the *Socialist Revolutionaries*, the Peasants' party. He was an able and energetic man who had been busy in the days of the revolution. He had saved one of the Tsar's ministers from an angry mob with the cry 'The Duma does not shed blood', and, with the aid of two soldiers with fixed bayonets, marched another former minister through a crowd saying firmly 'Do not touch this man.' A little later he arrived at a meeting of the Duma committee and threw a bundle of papers on the table and said that they were the secret *treaties* between Russia and her allies. His colleagues were baffled, and could think of no place to hide the papers, till someone suggested they put them under the tablecloth. While they were working this out Kerensky went off and returned with a box containing two million *roubles* which he had got in a government office. Kerensky was important because he was a member both of the Provisional Government and the Petrograd Soviet. Many workers and soldiers thought that the Soviet was a better group of people to rule the country than Provisional Government and many of the government's orders could be carried out only if the Soviet agreed. Kerensky's power was increased because he helped in making the decisions by which Russia was governed (in the Provisional Government) and in deciding whether these decisions would be carried out (in the Petrograd Soviet). The Soviet forced the government to arrest the Tsar and his family who were put under guard at Tsarskoye Selo. In August they were sent to Tobolsk in Siberia and then, in April 1918, the Bolsheviks sent them to Ekaterinburg. Throughout many parts of Russia it was local Soviets rather than the Provisional Government who gave the orders. Indeed, in some places the Provisional

Alexander Kerensky in the grounds of the Palace of Tsarskoye Selo, after the Tsar's abdication

Below: Tsar Nicholas II with his son Alexis, his daughter Tatiana and Prince Nikita (a cousin) under arrest at Tsarskoye Selo

Government was largely ignored, especially by the peasants who had begun seizing land from the landlords and by the soldiers who were deserting in order to join in. These were the men who, Lenin said, were 'voting for peace with their legs'. Now at last we meet the man in the title to this book. Who was he?

The Ulyanov family in 1879 at Simbrisk. Lenin is at the extreme right

5 Lenin in Exile

'Lenin' is a pen-name which has stuck. The man we call Lenin was born Vladimir Illyich Ulyanov in the town of Simbirsk on the Volga (Simbirsk was the birthplace of Alexander Kerensky also). His father was a school inspector and fairly well-off. Lenin was born in 1870 and had two brothers and three sisters. He lived in a large wooden house which had a fine garden and an apple and cherry orchard. As a small child Lenin was noisy and bad-tempered; he particularly liked smashing toys—his own or those of his friends. He was stocky and had a large head, so that people called him 'little barrel'. He was devoted to his elder brother 'Sasha' (short for Alexander).

He was very intelligent and an able pupil. He helped his fellow pupils, showing them how to translate difficult bits of Greek or German or solving problems in mathematics for them. When the examination results were given out he would run past his father's door and shout out the grades he had been given: 'Greek excellent, German excellent, Algebra excellent.'

In 1887, when Lenin was seventeen, his beloved brother Sasha was hanged for taking part in a plot to assassinate Tsar Alexander III (Sasha had made the bombs which were to have been used, but the secret police captured the plotters before the attempt was made). Lenin was shocked and saddened by his brother's death, but he said only: 'We must find another way.'

Lenin went to the University of Kazan, but was soon expelled. He and many other young Russians were protesting at the strictness of the Tsar's rule and it was decided to make some of them leave Kazan. A policeman spoke to Lenin as he led him to the edge of the city:

'Why did you engage in this revolt, young man? Don't you realise you're up against a wall?'

Yes, a wall, but a rotten one; one kick and it will crumble,' Lenin replied.

Lenin in 1892 when he was 22 years old

Lenin was exiled to his grandfather's estate where he went hunting, but rarely shot anything. He did not like killing animals and refused to shoot a fox 'because it was so beautiful'. Between 1889 and 1892 he trained to be a lawyer at Samara, and while he was there began to study the ideas of Karl Marx. When Marx died in 1883 his friend and *co-author* Friedrich Engels said in a speech at his graveside in Highgate Cemetery, London: 'On the afternoon of the fourteenth March at a quarter to three, the greatest living thinker ceased to think.'

Kark Marx was a German who spent most of his life (for a large part of which he was in London) working to produce a *revolution* which would change completely the way men lived. Marx did not go around bomb-throwing, actively trying to kill rulers or overthrow governments; instead, he was a thinker who in many writings, especially the *Communist Manifesto* and *Das Kapital*, set out his ideas and hoped to persuade other men to carry them out. His ideas were very complicated and men are still arguing over what he meant by some of the things he said and wrote. But the main ideas were these:

Firstly, Marx was a keen student of history and he was convinced that he had discovered a way to understand the past and, more important, to *predict* the future. He argued that history was a story of clashes or conflicts between *classes*, that is, large groups of people who had roughly similar incomes, ideas, ways of behaving and the like. The next great clash, he said, would be between the *capitalists*, the men who owned the factories and banks and railways etc.—those, that is, who employed other men—and the *proletariat*, the working class who were employed in the factories, on the railways etc. Marx believed that this great struggle would be won by the working class. Thereafter, the class system would be swept away, for there would be one class only—the working class. There would be no more class struggles and a way of living called *communism* would result—every one would work for the benefit of every one else and each would be given his fair share of what was produced—'to each according to his need; from each according to his ability'.

Secondly, by looking at the way men earned their living, Marx argued that the value of anything a man had made in the course of his work depended on how much work he had put into it. But, said Marx, the worker was paid only a fraction of the value of the goods he had produced (only enough, in fact, to keep himself and his family alive) while the remainder went to the employer. He went on to state that the workers would get poorer and poorer until they were so discontented that they would revolt against their employers—so here we are back again at the idea of a class-struggle between workers and employers. Now, many of Marx's ideas proved to be incorrect, but they were so ably argued that they persuaded many people that they might be true. And the man who was influenced by Marx perhaps more than any other, was Lenin.

In 1893 Lenin went to St Petersburg. He had been so caught up by Marx's ideas that he decided to give his life to bringing about the revolution which Marx had predicted. Lenin joined

Newly built statue to Karl Marx and Friedrich Engels shortly after the Bolshevik revolution

a group who shared Marx's ideas, and began to show what a great leader he would make. He had immense knowledge; he was a tough debater (someone who had argued with him came away saying that it was as though he had been hit over the head with a flail!); he worked tremendously hard; he was very strong-willed and simply refused to take obstacles seriously. He wrote an enormous amount (perhaps some 10 million words—this book contains about 20,000). He was sent to prison in 1895 because of some of his writings which the Tsar's government disapproved of. While in prison he wrote part of a book and played chess: the prisoners worked out a special code of taps and tapped out the moves from cell to cell. A year later Lenin was sent into exile in Siberia. There he lived in a peasant's hut on the banks of the Yenesai. Exile was not very strict and Lenin was joined by his fiancée Nadezhda Krupskaya, whom he married in 1898. In 1900 Lenin was allowed to leave Russia and he went to live in western Europe, staying for a time in London (at 30 Holford Square). There were a number of Russian groups who opposed the government of the Tsars. One of these was the group of the Socialist Revolutionaries, who believed that the peasants were the people in Russia on whom everything depended, and who hoped for a Russia in which everyone had a vote and the land was owned by the peasants. The other main group was the *Social Democrats*, whose ideas were based on those of Karl Marx. They thought that a revolution in Russia must come from the workers in the towns. In 1903 the Social Democrats held a meeting in London and an argument arose over who were to be allowed to become members of the party. One group favoured allowing anyone who declared himself a supporter to join; the other group (Lenin's) said that only those completely devoted to the party and determined to work hard for it should be allowed in. Lenin's group won the vote by a small majority and Lenin thereafter called his group by the Russian word for a majority group—Bolsheviks; while the others were called *Mensheviks* (minority party). This split showed one important thing about Lenin: he was determined to have his own way.

In the years before 1917 Lenin and the Bolsheviks achieved very little. Lenin spent most of his time abroad living in various European cities. He wrote incessantly and made plans for the revolution which he expected would happen eventually. In 1914 he moved to Switzerland when the First World War began. He was still in Switzerland in 1917.

6 To the Finland Station

In January 1917 Lenin had made a speech to a group of Swiss working men. He said that a great revolution would take place in Russia, but he felt that it would not happen soon, indeed probably not in his lifetime. Two months later, however, a Polish friend rushed into the flat in Zurich where Lenin and Krupskaya were living. 'Haven't you heard the news?' the friend asked excitedly. 'There's been a revolution in Russia.'

The news of the February Revolution had taken a week to arrive in Switzerland and at first Lenin could not believe it. He and Krupskaya hurried down to the lakeside where the newspapers were displayed as soon as they came out. It was true! Lenin realised, as he read the stories of fighting in Petrograd, that a revolution was taking place, and he was angry with himself for being so far away from Russia when it was happening. 'I am preparing to leave and am packing my bags', he wrote to a friend. Lenin was sure that a second revolution would follow the first, and he wanted to play a part in that. However, he soon realised that it would not be easy to get back to Russia. Switzerland's neighbours were Germany (at war with Russia) and France and Italy (fighting on Russia's side). Lenin feared that if he tried to travel through Germany he would be arrested for being a Russian; while if he travelled through France he might well be arrested for being a Bolshevik—for it was well known that the Bolsheviks wanted Russia to withdraw from the war, and the French naturally wanted Russia to remain in it; they might therefore try to prevent Lenin from returning to Russia. For a time, 41 therefore, Lenin felt that he would not be able to leave 'this accursed Switzerland', and so he sent his orders to the Russian Bolsheviks by letter.

Then he changed his mind: he would try to get back to Russia. He thought up plan after plan and became so restless that he could not sleep. His first idea was to fly across Germany to Russia, but no suitable aircraft existed (even if Lenin had been able to borrow or steal it). His next idea was that he and Zinoviev, a Bolshevik colleague, should borrow Swedish passports and use these to return to Russia. Neither, unfortunately, could speak any Swedish, so Lenin proposed that they should pretend to be deaf mutes!

An even more ridiculous idea came to him: he would get help from his friend Karpinsky, a librarian in Geneva, to whom he wrote a most odd letter:

'Please *procure* in your name papers for travelling to France and England, and I will use them when passing through England and Holland to Russia. I can wear a wig. . . . You must then disappear from Geneva for at least two or three weeks (until you receive a telegram from me in Scandinavia). During that time you must be extremely careful and go into hiding in the mountains, where we shall of course pay for your board and lodging.'

At last someone realised that since the Bolsheviks were against the war the Germans might be quite willing to help their leader to return to Russia. If Lenin managed somehow to withdraw Russia from the war, Germany could then put almost all her soldiers on the Western Front against Britain and France. The Germans therefore agreed to send Lenin and some of his friends and colleagues through Germany on the way to Russia. They were to travel in a 'sealed' train; that is, the Russians were to have no contact with the Germans who were manning the train. The main reason for this was that some of the Bolsheviks were afraid that if they spoke to the Germans they might be charged with treason when they reached Russia.

There were just over thirty passengers in the special train

Route of Lenin's return to Russia

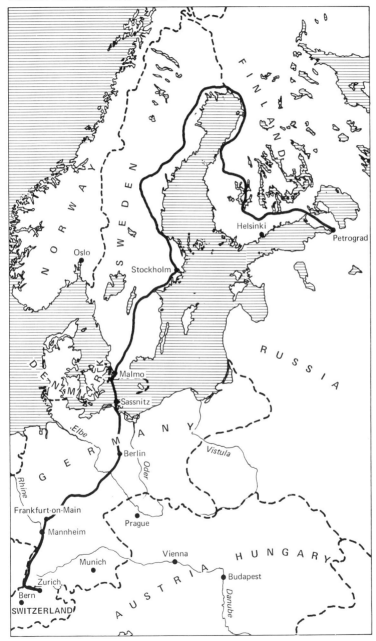

which set off from Switzerland on 27 March, 1917. The passengers had brought their luggage in paper parcels and string bags; food for ten days was already aboard. The journey had almost ended before it had begun at the station, when a number of Russian exiles, thinking that Lenin and his friends were being bribed by the Germans, nearly caused a riot. The Bolsheviks sang their song, the 'Internationale' amid shouts of 'German spies', and 'The Kaiser is paying for the journey.' There were scuffles on the platform in which Lenin's umbrella came in useful. Finally, after a stowaway had been thrown off, the train began its journey.

The travellers were very well fed (mainly because the Germans were trying to convince them that Germany had plenty of food and was not suffering from the *blockade*), and they were supplied with vast quantities of newspapers and beer.

Lenin tried to work during the journey, but was disturbed by his companions singing and joking. The train was held up for a time in Berlin because some German had mislaid the telegram which had given the Bolsheviks permission to go through Sweden. At length they set off for the Baltic coast and crossed by ferryboat into Sweden. In Stockholm Lenin bought himself a new hat. Another train took the travellers from Sweden to Finland and they crossed the frontier on sleighs. They were now in Russian territory and had to fill up an entry form. Here is Lenin's:

FOR RUSSIAN SUBJECTS ARRIVING FROM ABROAD THROUGH FRONTIER STATION OF TORNIO

2 April *(O.S.)*, 1917.

Name, patronymic, surname, rank:

Vladimir Ilyich Ulyanov

Last residence:

Stockholm (Sweden) (Hotel Regina, Stockholm)

Age, nationality, religion:

Born 10 April (O.S.), 1870 at Simbirsk; Russian Orthodox

For what purpose did you go abroad?:

Political refugee. Left Russia illegally

Give address and purpose of visit if stopping in Finland:

No intention of stopping.

To what city are you going? Give address:
Petrograd. Sister's address: Mariya Illyichna
Ulyanova, Shirokaya St. 48/9, Apt. 24.
Profession:
Journalist
Signature: Vladimir Ulyanov

Lenin and his friends were admitted without difficulty and another train took them off to Petrograd. Lenin had half expected to be arrested when the train pulled into Petrograd's Finland Station. Instead, a huge Bolshevik demonstration had been planned. As Lenin stepped from the train a band played the 'Marseillaise': Lenin seemed both astonished and embarrassed by the reception, for he hated ceremonies. He and the leaders of the reception went into what had been the Tsar's waiting room. Speeches were made while Lenin awkwardly fingered the bouquet of red roses he had been given.

Then some soldiers burst into the room and lifted Lenin on their shoulders to carry him to the station square. Searchlights shone, bands played, banners were waved, and the name 'Lenin! Lenin!' was chanted by the crowd.

Lenin climbed on to the turret of an armoured car, his coat open, the new hat stuffed into his pocket. A searchlight picked him out. He waited for silence and then spoke briefly. The February Revolution, he said, had freed Russia from the Tsar. The next task was to bring about a second revolution which would give control of Russia to the workers and peasants and lead to other such revolutions everywhere. The crowd roared approval. Lenin looked around him with satisfaction. After ten long years of exile he had returned to Russia, and to what a welcome!

7 The July Days and Kornilov

The Provisional Government made some changes in the way Russia was governed. The Russian people were given far more freedom than they had had under the Tsars—there were no secret police to watch them, and men were no longer sent off to Siberia. Indeed, many of the exiles were allowed to return to Russia, and the most famous of these, Lenin, admitted when he returned, that of all the countries fighting in the First World War, Russia was the freest. But the government got little thanks for what it did; like most returning exiles, Lenin showed no gratitude to it and people complained more about what the government did not do. It did little, for example, for the various national groups in Russia who wanted more control of their own affairs. The Finns were given some more freedom and the Poles were given *independence* (since most of Poland had been conquered by Germany this made no difference to anyone!), but most were ignored, and some therefore got very angry, especially the 'Little Russians' or Ukranians. The peasants, too, were unhappy, because the Provisional Government would do nothing about the land. And the workers were the most dissatisfied of all. They tended to ignore the government altogether and when they wanted anything asked the Soviet for it (getting, for example, an eight-hour day).

However, the Provisional Government's greatest mistake was their decision to undertake a great attack or offensive in June 1917 under the command of General Brusilov. Great preparations were made; special '*battalions* of death' (some composed of women) were formed to set an example of bravery to the others, and Kerensky (now the minister in charge of the war) went around making speeches to inspire the soldiers. They clapped and cheered him when he had spoken, but went on talking about peace when he left.

The attack was successful at first, but when more and more German troops arrived on the battlefields the Russians were stopped, then forced to retreat in great disorder. The losses of men were very heavy. One Russian general, Kornilov, even began machine-gunning deserting soldiers to try to make them stand and fight. But it was too late: the Russian army's fighting spirit was gone, and the retreat stopped only because the Germans gave up the chase.

Meanwhile, Lenin had been very busy. Most of the Bolsheviks had been in exile at the time of the February Revolution, and so the party had done little then. Indeed they were uncertain whether they should support the Provisional

Lenin

Government and whether they should be in favour of the war or not. Lenin had no doubts. The day after his arrival at the Finland Station he announced to his fellow Bolsheviks his 'April Theses'. The Bolsheviks should not support the Provisional Government, he argued; the Soviet should govern Russia. The Soviet should then take over all the land and the banks. The war should be stopped as soon as possible; meanwhile the Russian soldiers should be encouraged to make friends with the German soldiers in the trenches.

People were astonished by the April Theses. One Menshevik said that Lenin must have gone mad, and even the Bolshevik newspaper *Pravda* said that Lenin had not understood what had happened in Russia in the last two months. Some Bolsheviks, however, agreed with Lenin. One who did so was a young man from Georgia in south Russia called Stalin. His father was a poor cobbler but his mother saved hard to send him to college to be a priest. But Stalin secretly studied Marxism, tried to organise a protest among some oil workers, and was exiled to Siberia. He escaped and worked hard for the Bolsheviks, writing articles for papers and raising money by carrying out daring and violent bank robberies. He seemed to be dull and few people thought he was very clever (one man said that in 1917 Stalin moved about like a 'grey blur'), but he believed firmly in Lenin's ideas. Lenin himself fought hard in speeches and newspaper articles to convince his party that he was right. His arguments were direct and clear, and all could understand him. He found simple words which appealed to many people—'end the war', 'all land to the peasants', 'all power to the Soviets', and gradually his followers accepted the April Theses. Support for Lenin's ideas came, too, from Leon Trotsky, a Menshevik who had been in exile in America. He and Lenin had quarrelled in the past (Lenin once called him a 'windbag'), but in 1917 Trotsky was sure that Lenin's plan was the right one, and he won support for Lenin by effective speeches to soldiers and workers. He soon joined the Bolshevik party himself.

The Bolsheviks were a fairly small party, but they were

Above: Stalin's record card and photographs from the files of the Okhrana, (1912–3)

Leon Trotsky, 1917

49

stronger than most because they stuck together and had a lot of faith in themselves and their leader. In June a meeting of the people from Soviets throughout Russia was held. Only one *delegate* in every eight was a Bolshevik, yet when a speaker said that the Provisional Government alone could rule Russia since no one else was willing to say 'Give us power', Lenin stood and said 'Yes, there is!' and when he was jeered at, he replied 'Laugh as much as you like'.

Yet when the Bolsheviks seemed to be getting more and more followers in the army and factories things suddenly went wrong for them during the 'July days'. Some Petrograd workers, annoyed that they were no better off than under the Tsars and angry at the failure of the Brusilov offensive, marched through Petrograd. There was some shooting and marchers killed people they thought were *sniping* at them. The marchers were trying to persuade the Soviet to take over from the Provisional Government—just what the Bolsheviks had been saying for months. The Bolsheviks were very unhappy, because they felt that a rising against the government at this time was a mistake, yet they felt they had to support the workers who were using their *slogans*. Kerensky, however, persuaded some of the troops in Petrograd that the Bolsheviks were German agents and the rising soon fizzled out. The offices and printing machinery of 'Pravda' were smashed up, and a warrant was issued for Lenin's arrest. Lenin wanted to stay and stand trial, but his friends feared he would be murdered in prison and he fled to Finland where the Russian police could not follow him. The Bolshevik party seemed to be finished.

Suddenly they had a stroke of luck. Kersensky, who had nearly destroyed the party, was the man who gave it the chance to recover. He had by this time become Prime Minister when Prince Lvov resigned. He felt he must get as much support from the people as possible, since they were blaming him for the failure of the offensive. In August he called a meeting in the Bolshoi Theatre of 2,500 people from all sorts of groups —the Duma, the army and trade unions, the Soviets and so on.

Lenin addressing the crowd, 1917. Trotsky is standing beside the platform

A crowd dispersed by shooting during the July Days

When the meeting was held many of the richer delegates did not support him. The factory owners were worried because more and more workers were supporting the Bolsheviks (largely because prices were rising and there was dreadful hunger, so that children were 'dying like flies'). They demanded more money and if the employers refused and closed the factories, the workers sometimes reopened them. These wealthy men had never been happy about the revolution, and many of them wanted to see the Soviets swept away and a strong government like that of the Tsar set up. The man they wanted to lead this government was General Kornilov. He was very brave and strong but stupid. Brusilov said of him

General Kornilov

that he was 'a man with the heart of a lion and the brains of a lamb'. He had been born in Siberia and was always accompanied by a bodyguard of *Caucasian* cavalrymen clad in long red cloaks. By this time he had been made commander-in-chief of the army and when he appeared in the Bolshoi he was showered with blossoms by the richer delegates. He suggested that one answer to Russia's problems was to use army discipline in the factories (and a soldier could, of course, be shot for refusing to obey orders). He got louder cheers than Kerensky. When he returned to the front he left one of his officers, General Krymov, near Petrograd with a force of Caucasians and Cossacks, giving orders that they were to deal with the Bolsheviks if they gave any more trouble. Kornilov told one of his officers: 'It's time to hang the German supporters and spies with Lenin at their head and to *disperse* the Soviet.'

Then Kerensky learned of a plan which would have made Kornilov the ruler of Russia. Kerensky realised that he was in terrible danger, so he turned to the party he knew would fight Kornilov to the death—the Bolsheviks. The Petrograd workers were given rifles, and sailors from Kronstadt arrived to help. Under Bolshevik leadership trenches were dug and barbed wire strung across streets. Railway workers were sent orders to block tracks (they tipped over carriages or tore up rails), and they cleverly switched the trains carrying Krymov's troops to quiet sidings where they were cut off from the others. Bolsheviks and others arrived among the troops to persuade them not to fight against Petrograd and in the Soviet some Caucasians were found to go and convince their fellow country-men not to follow Kornilov. They were so successful that the Caucasians sent a message of apology to the Petrograd Soviet. Krymov himself went to Petrograd, had an angry talk with Kerensky, and then shot himself. Kornilov had been ill with fever and unable to do anything. He was taken prisoner, and his plan to rule Russia collapsed. But everyone knew that those who had done most to bring this about were the Bolsheviks.

8 Soldiers, Peasants, Workers

General Kornilov had tried to capture Petrograd and make himself ruler of Russia, but he had failed. Alexander Kerensky was still Prime Minister, but many people no longer trusted him. They thought that he and Kornilov had been plotting together, and Kerensky foolishly made things worse for himself by letting Kornilov's bodyguards act as his prison warders.

Some of the Russian generals were very unpopular too: while they had been helping Kornilov the Germans had captured the Russian city of Riga.

Meanwhile Lenin and his Bolsheviks had become much more popular. They had fought hard to defend Petrograd and had talked hard to persuade Kornilov's soldiers not to fight. The Bolshevik soldiers, the Red Guard, had been given guns when Petrograd was in danger. They kept their guns afterwards and Lenin thus had a private army of factory workers.

Early in September the Bolsheviks became the most powerful group in the Moscow and Petrograd Soviets. Since the members of these councils were directly elected by the people and the soldiers, it was clear that more and more people were supporting Lenin. The Bolsheviks were very skilful in their speeches and slogans and in one of these they promised exactly what most Russians wanted: 'Peace; land to the peasants; workers' control in industry; all power to the Soviets.' Thus they managed in a very few words to appeal to the three main groups of ordinary Russians in 1917: soldiers, peasants and factory workers.

There were 9 million men in the Russian army in 1917 and
most were sure that the war should be ended. They felt that

the Government should make peace, but if it did not, then the soldiers should refuse to fight. The soldiers had suffered for years. They had been led by foolish officers; had had too little food and not enough equipment or ammunition, and there had been millions of casualties. Though they were brave they no longer wanted to fight. Since the February Revolution *discipline* had been breaking down, especially as officers mainly opposed the revolution while most soldiers supported it. Russian soldiers began to disobey orders; drunkenness and riots against food shortages became common and large numbers of soldiers deserted (some even *commandeered* trains and made for home). Some unpopular officers were beaten or even *lynched* and grenades were on occasion lobbed into officer's quarters. The Provisional Government was thus losing control over its soldiers and by the time the Bolsheviks were ready to try to seize power in October 1917, the government's supporters included only some Cossacks and some officer *cadets*, and a women's battalion.

Meanwhile the Bolsheviks had been working hard to win

Russian deserters returning home, 1917

support among the soldiers. One soldier wrote in August:

'Our Provisional Government attacks the Bolsheviks very much, but we front line soldiers don't find any fault in them. Earlier we were against the Bolsheviks, but now, after the Provisional Government has promised to give freedom to the poor people, and hasn't given it, we are little by little passing over to the side of the Bolsheviks.'

The Bolsheviks were particularly successful in winning the friendship of most of the Petrograd *garrison;* this turned out to be very important later.

'Land to the peasants', the second part of the Bolshevik slogan, appealed to the four-fifths of the Russian people who lived in the countryside. Most Russian peasants were poor, partly because their ways of farming were old-fashioned, partly because they usually grew only one crop and of course if it failed, because of disease or bad weather, they were in great trouble. The peasants thought, however, that the reason for their troubles was that the landlords had too much land and demanded too high a rent. Many peasants had a simple answer: seize the land from the landlord and stop paying rent! The war made things worse for the peasants. Twelve million peasants (and two million farm horses) were taken into the army, so that those left at home, the weaker and the older, had to work harder than before. Things were no better after the February Revolution, so the peasants began to tackle their problems themselves. Rents were unpaid, animals were pastured on the lords' lands, landlords' granaries were broken into. Gradually, the peasants became more violent—lords' lands were seized, the 'Red Cock' (fire) was turned loose on their houses, some lords were murdered. Kerensky tried to crush the peasants as a Tsar would have done—but he could not get the troops to act against the peasants, whom he annoyed but could not restrain. Once again the Bolsheviks benefited—the peasants were doing what they said should be done. If the Bolsheviks should seize power they need not fear any trouble from the peasants, while the peasants would not lift a finger to save the Provisional Government.

However, the Bolsheviks needed more than people who would not oppose them; they had to have real supporters if they were to seize the government of Russia. And in the summer and autumn of 1917 Lenin's Bolsheviks by careful persuasion got the help they had been seeking: their allies were the factory workers of the great cities, especially Moscow and Petrograd. Karl Marx had believed that the factory workers were the people who would make revolutions. In the 'Communist Manifesto' he had written: 'The proletariat alone is really revolutionary.' Marx wrote these words in 1848 and was not thinking of Russia when he did so, for Russia had few factory workers at that time. Gradually, however, factories had been built. The worker's ghastly conditions became almost unbearable during the war as supplies of food and fuel broke down, and the February Revolution did nothing to help them.

John Reed, an American journalist was in Petrograd in 1917. He watched many of the great events which occurred in

A meeting of peasants in a Russian village to decide how to distribute the landowners' land among themselves, April, 1917

the city and wrote a famous book 'Ten Days that Shook the World' (Reed died in 1920 and was buried in Red Square, Moscow), in which he tells the story of the Bolshevik Revolution. He gives us this description of Petrograd in the autumn of 1917:

'September and October are the worst months of the Russian year—especially the Petrograd year. Under dull grey skies, in the shortening days, the rain fell drenching, incessant. The mud underfoot was deep, slippery and clinging, tracked everywhere by heavy boots. . . . Bitter damp winds rushed in from the Gulf of Finland, and the chill fog rolled through the streets. At night, for motives of economy as well as fear of *Zeppelins*, the street-lights were few and far between.

'It was dark from three in the afternoon till ten in the morning. Robberies and house-breaking increased. In apartment houses the men took turns at all-night guard duty, armed with loaded rifles.

'Week by week food became scarcer. The daily allowance of bread fell. . . . Towards the end there was a week without any bread at all. Sugar, one was entitled to at the rate of two pounds per month—if one could get it at all, which was seldom. A bar of chocolate . . . cost anywhere from seven to ten roubles—at least a dollar. There was milk for about half the babies in the city; most hotels and private houses never saw it for months.

'For milk and bread and sugar and tobacco one had to stand in a queue long hours in the chill rain.'

The workers like the peasants began to act to improve their situation after February. Some managed to get shorter working hours and higher wages. Strikes became more violent and many workers were angered by a remark uttered by a famous factory owner: 'Perhaps we need the bony hand of hunger, the poverty of the people, which would seize by the throats all these friends of the people . . . all these Soviets. . . .'

Some managers were beaten (and one was carried from his factory in a wheelbarrow), some were killed. The Provisional

Government, as usual, was unable to do anything to improve matters, and the workers began to try to get control of the factories in which they worked. Some argued that Russia should be governed by the Soviets. This was what the Bolsheviks were saying should happen, so the Bolsheviks found allies in the workers. Moreover, the workers were quite prepared to overthrow the Provisional Government. The Bolsheviks then had the force they needed to try to gain control of the country. Would they make the effort to do so?

9 Lenin Persuades the Bolsheviks

Lenin, of course, was still in exile in Finland but he knew what was happening in Russia. He knew that the soldiers and peasants were not unfriendly to his Bolsheviks, and that factory workers were prepared to help them. He knew also that the Bolsheviks themselves were becoming stronger: more people were joining them. Meanwhile the government was growing weaker: the soldiers and peasants distrusted it, the workers detested it. Its leader, Alexander Kerensky, was a gifted man but he often seemed unable to make up his mind what to do. Lenin, however, was absolutely sure: the Bolsheviks should

Lenin's forged passport with which he escaped to Finland in 1917 after the July Days

overthrow the Provisional Government and gain control of Russia for themselves, then a *socialist* state could be established.

The most important Bolsheviks were in the Central Committee which decided what the party would or would not do. The members of the Central Committee were mainly people who had given long and able service to the party; many had been in the Tsar's prisons, and *labour camps;* several had spent many years in exile, only returning when the February Revolution had taken place. It was the Central Committee that Lenin had to convince. Lenin used all his powers of argument, all his vast knowledge and fierce determination to overthrow a government which he considered was solely there to help the middle classes whom he despised (though he was, of course, of middle-class family himself). On 10 October Lenin, who had come to Petrograd disguised in wig and beard, met the other eleven members of the Central Committee at a house in the city. Few more important meetings have ever been held. From early evening until the early hours of the following morning the debate continued, while the debaters kept themselves going on sausage, sandwiches and cups of tea. At last the vote was taken, and Lenin's view—that the Bolsheviks should act, should try to seize power immediately—was carried by ten votes to two. Those supporting Lenin included Trotsky and Stalin; the two who voted against him were Zinoviev and Kamenev. The Central Committee had decided and the other Bolsheviks were secretly told. The actual work of planning the revolt was done by a small group of men in the Petrograd Soviet led by Trotsky. However, before they had even begun to prepare, Lenin had to crush an effort made by Zinoviev and Kamenev to stop the revolt—indeed, they went so far as to write in a newspaper that the Bolsheviks were planning to overthrow the government and that they, Zinoviev and Kamenev, felt that this was a mistake! Lenin would have none of it. The Bolsheviks, he said, must strike immediately. 'Hunger does not wait. The peasant uprising does not wait. The war does not wait.' There was no more trouble from Zinoviev and Kamenev, and Trotsky made his preparations.

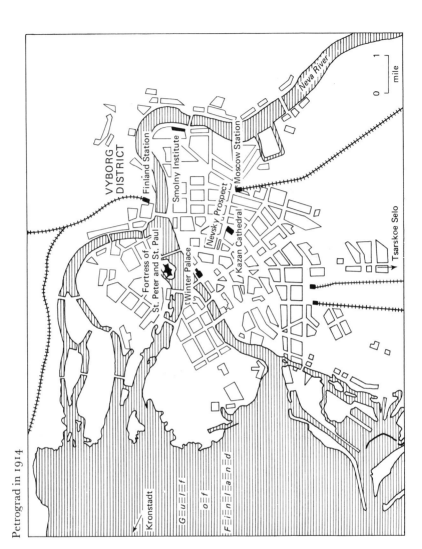

Petrograd in 1914

VYBORG DISTRICT

Finland Station

Smolny Institute

Moscow Station

Neva River

Nevsky Prospect

Kazan Cathedral

Tsarskoe Selo

Fortress of St. Peter and St. Paul

Winter Palace

Kronstadt

Gulf of Finland

0   1
mile

62

10 The Bolshevik Revolution

The Bolsheviks had a stroke of luck. The Provisional Government decided to send some of the soldiers guarding Petrograd to fight against Germany. The Bolsheviks protested and the troops stayed in Petrograd. Naturally, the soldiers were grateful to the Bolsheviks and annoyed at the government, who thus lost any hope of support from the troops guarding the capital.

Meanwhile there was tremendous activity in the Bolshevik headquarters, the Smolny Institute, as John Reed vividly describes:

'Smolny Institute . . . lay miles out on the edge of the city, beside the wide Neva. I went there on a *street-car*, moving snail-like with a groaning noise through the cobbled, muddy streets, jammed with people. . . . Once a famous convent school for the daughters of the Russian nobility . . . the Institute had been taken over by . . . the workers and soldiers. . . .

The long *vaulted* corridors, lit by rare electric lights, were thronged with hurrying shapes of soldiers and workmen, some bent under the weight of huge bundles of newspapers, *proclamations*, printed *propaganda* of all sorts. The sound of their heavy boots made a deep thunder on the wooden floor. . . . Signs were posted up everywhere: "Comrades: for the sake of your health, preserve cleanliness!"

'For two roubles I bought a ticket entitling me to dinner, and stood in line with a thousand others, waiting to get to the long serving tables where twenty men and women were ladling from immense *cauldrons* cabbage soup, hunks of meat and slabs of black bread. Five *kopeks* paid for tea in a tin cup. From a basket one grabbed a greasy wooden spoon. . . . The benches along the wooden tables were packed with hungry workers, wolfing their food, plotting, shouting rough jokes across the room.'

The Bolsheviks of course tried to build up support from the ordinary people of Petrograd. Speakers were sent out to different districts and to factories all over the city. On 22 October Trotsky spoke at a series of meetings whose aim was to show the people 'their own numbers, their own strength' and, of course, to gain support for a revolt. In his speech Trotsky said:

'The Soviet Government will give everything that is in the country to the poor and to the people in the trenches. You well-to-do folk have two coats—hand one over to the soldiers who are cold in the trenches. You have warm boots? Sit at home; the worker needs your boots.'

The effect of these words on the hungry, poorly clad Petrograd worker, especially in the cold, damp bleak days of autumn, is not hard to imagine. Perhaps he did not believe that Trotsky and the Bolsheviks would do all they said. But at least they promised to do something, while the Provisional Government

did nothing and did not seem to care for anyone.

On 23 October the Provisional Government lost one of its main strongholds. On an island on the River Neva lay the important fortress of St Peter and St Paul. Its guns were within easy range of the Winter Palace where the government had its headquarters, and in its *arsenal* there was a large supply of arms. Trotsky visited the fortress and found a meeting of its garrison in progress. He spoke to the troops and persuaded them to support the Bolsheviks, who thus gained control of a vital fortress and a large number of weapons for the Red Guard.

There was great activity that evening. At the Smolny there was much coming and going as men were sent out on various tasks and others arrived with news of happenings in various parts of the city.

At last Kerensky decided to do something and the Provisional Government tried to take counter-measures against the Bolsheviks. Kerensky's only reliable force were the officer cadets or *junkers* and he decided to use them to close down the Bolshevik newspapers and arrest the leading Bolsheviks. Also he sent a battalion of women soldiers to help defend the Winter Palace and ordered the cruiser 'Aurora', which was anchored

The Women's Battalion in front of the Winter Palace
Left: Queuing for potatoes, October, 1917

in the Neva and was well known to support the Bolsheviks, to put to sea. Lastly, the junkers took over important points in the city—railway stations, bridges etc.

But Kerensky was too late. The Red Guards reopened the newspapers; the 'Aurora' remained at anchor and on the evening of 24 October the Bolsheviks settled the last details of their revolt.

At 2 a.m. on the morning of 25 October 1917 the Bolshevik Revolution, one of the most important events in the history of the world, began. As usual John Reed was an eye witness. At the Smolny he met a friend.

> ' "We're moving!" he said calmly . . . "we pinched the assistant Minister of Justice and the Minister of Religions. They're down in the cellar now. One regiment is on the march to capture the Telephone Exchange, another the Telegraph Agency, another the State Bank. The Red Guard is out. . . ."
>
> 'On the steps of Smolny in the chill dark we first saw the Red Guards—a huddled group of boys in workmen's clothes, carrying guns with bayonets, talking nervously together.
>
> 'Far over the still roofs westward came the sound of scattered rifle fire, where the junkers were trying to prevent the factory workers and soldiers of the Viborg quarter from joining the Soviet forces in the centre of the city. . . .
>
> 'Behind us, great Smolny, bright with lights hummed like a gigantic hive. . . .'

Bolshevik forces thus rapidly occupied the important places of Petrograd—the railway stations, bridges, the State Bank and the main telephone exchange. There was little bloodshed, and the Bolshevik forces, mainly Red Guards and sailors from the Baltic fleet, easily overcame the junkers—who were greatly outnumbered and not too keen to fight anyway.

Meanwhile life went on calmly in Petrograd, even though a great revolution was taking place. Cinemas and theatres remained open, shops continued to serve their customers, tram-

cars ran as usual.

Junkers in the Winter Palace just before the Bolshevik attack, October, 1917

Armed sentries guard a post office against Bolsheviks, October, 1917

Kerensky, of course, was trying desperately to fight off the Bolsheviks, but could count on few trustworthy soldiers. Even the Cossacks, who had for so long served the Tsar, were unwilling to fight. (They sent numerous messages that they were 'getting ready to saddle their horses', but they never actually mounted.) Kerensky therefore decided to go off to the front to try to secure *reinforcements*, and managed to slip through the Bolshevik patrols in a car borrowed from the American Embassy and flying the Stars and Stripes. What was left of the Provisional Government held out in the Winter Palace, hoping that Kerensky would return with aid.

By the afternoon the Bolsheviks controlled all Petrograd except the Winter Palace. In the early evening they demanded the surrender of the Palace but this *ultimatum* was rejected, and so plans were made to assault the building. Many of the defenders had quietly slipped away, leaving only the junkers and the women's battalion to protect the members of the Government. They made barriers from firewood and prepared for a siege. The Bolsheviks brought up armoured cars and forces of Red Guards. The 'Aurora' fired a few shells, but did little damage. The women's battalion attempted to come out and fight, was surrounded, and surrendered. There were *volleys* of rifle and machine-gun fire. At length groups of Red Guards began to break into the vast building—it occupies four-and-half acres—and skirmished with the junkers. Each side was a bit unsure of itself. One Red Guard, seeing the reflection of the painting of a horseman in a large mirror, gave a frightened cry of 'the cavalry' and turned and fled. However, as vast crowds gathered around the palace, more and more Bolsheviks made their way in and disarmed the junkers. Finally the Bolsheviks reached the inner rooms where the Ministers were sheltering.

They decided to surrender, and the Bolsheviks military commander, Antonov Ovseyenko, 'a slight figure with a sharp face and a broad-brimmed hat', strode into the room and arrested the Ministers who were taken to the dungeons of St Peter and St Paul and soon released. Six Bolsheviks were killed

The cruiser *Aurora*

Bolshevik troops storming the Winter Palace

in the storming of the Winter Palace: none of the defenders died.

While the guns were firing on the Winter Palace a meeting of the Congress of Soviets was being held at Smolny. Most supported the Bolsheviks and those who didn't soon left with Trotsky's blistering words in their ears: 'You are miserable, isolated individuals. You are bankrupt. You have played out your role. Go where you belong: to the dustbin of history.'

On the next evening, 26 October, at the Congress of Soviets, Lenin announced the Bolshevik plans. John Reed describes the scene:

'It was just 8.40 when a thundering wave of cheers announced the entrance of the leaders, with Lenin—great Lenin—among them. A short, stocky figure, with a big head set down on his shoulders, bald and bulging. Little eyes, a snubbish nose, wide generous mouth, and heavy chin; clean shaven now but beginning to bristle with the well-known beard. . . . Dressed in shabby clothes, his trousers much too long for him. Unimpressive, to be the idol of a mob, loved and *revered* as perhaps few leaders in history have been.'

And then he rose to speak:

'Now Lenin, gripping the edge of the reading stand, letting his little winking eyes travel over the crowd as he stood there waiting, apparently *oblivious* to the long rolling *ovation*, which lasted several minutes.

'When it finished he said simply, "We shall now proceed to construct the *Socialist order*." Again that overwhelming roar.'

Then he announced two *decrees*—on peace and on land. He proposed that there should be immediate peace; no country should gain any land. This had no practical effect, of course, because the other countries which were fighting would have to be asked for their opinions, but Lenin's decision was very welcome to most Russians. The second decree proposed that all the land of Russia should be handed over to the peasants who should decide how to divide it up. 'Let the peasants decide all questions', he said. 'Let them organize their own life.' In fact, Lenin was unhappy about the peasants' plan—a large number of small farms; but he was prepared to accept the idea for a while to get peasant support for his government while it was new and not very strong. Next, Lenin gave the names of his ministers, who were to be called Commissars. Lenin was to be Chairman, Trotsky Commissar for Foreign Affairs, and Stalin Commissar for Nationalities (he was to look after all the non-Russians in the population of Russia).

The new government had to deal with very difficult problems. In some parts of Russia—the Ukraine and the Cossack lands of the Don and the Kuban—the Bolsheviks were unpopular and could expect to have to fight. Moreover, the Moscow Bolsheviks had shown less determination than their Petrograd comrades and had lost the Kremlin after having captured it. Worst of all, news came that Kerensky, who had made his way to Pskov, was advancing on Petrograd with a force of the dreaded Cossacks. By 28 October they were in Tsarskoye Selo, near Petrograd. Hurriedly the Red Guards dug trenches and strung barbed wire on the outskirts of the capital; volunteers arrived in taxis and tramcars to man the defences. As usual John Reed was there:

'As we came out into the dark and gloomy day all around the grey horizon factory whistles were blowing, a hoarse and nervous sound, full of foreboding. By tens of thousands the working people poured out, men and women. . . . Red Petrograd was in danger! Cossacks! South and south-west they poured through the shabby streets towards the Moskovsky Gate, men, women and children, with rifles, picks, spades, rolls of wire, cartridge belts over their working clothes. . . . They rolled along torrent like, companies of soldiers borne with them, guns, motor trucks and wagons.'

On 29 October some junkers seized the Petrograd telephone exchange and were thrown out only after fighting and much bloodshed.

The Bolsheviks looked as though they were going to be beaten, but Kerensky had only 700 men and was soon forced 71 back. Kerensky himself managed to escape, disguised as a sailor, and soon left Russia. (He reached Britain and now lives in the United States, the only one of the great men involved in the Revolutions of 1917 who is still alive.) The Red Guards in Moscow stormed the Kremlin, and in many parts of Russia the Bolsheviks soon fairly easily gained control.

By early November 1917, one week after the beginning of their Revolution, the Bolshevik party ruled most of Russia. Today, over fifty years later the Bolsheviks, now called the Communist Party of the Soviet Union, still rule Russia.

11 Peace

Though the Bolsheviks were in control of most of Russia there were many parts where their rule was not accepted. The three most important areas were around Kiev in the Ukraine, the Cossack lands near the Black Sea, and the area in western Russia around Mogilev. The Ukranians and Cossacks were to give the Bolsheviks much trouble, but the Mogilev area, where the commander-in-chief of the Russian armies, General Sukhovin, had his headquarters, was soon in Bolshevik hands. The general was beaten to death by a mob of soldiers, sailors and peasants. The Bolsheviks then took over control of the army.

The Bolsheviks found that it was very difficult to govern Russia. They had nearly all been revolutionaries and exiles and had had no experience of governing even a village, far less an immense country. Moreover, those who had this experience, the civil servants who had worked for the Tsars and the Provisional Government, detested the Bolsheviks and went on strike as a protest as soon as the Commissars arrived at their offices. Soldiers had to be used to make the civil servants hand over their keys and force the State Bank to give money to the Bolshevik Government. At length, however, the strike collapsed.

In spite of difficulties and lack of experience Lenin and his colleagues issued an immense number of laws for the reform of Russia: workers were to control their industries; banks were *nationalised*; debts to foreign countries were not to be paid; large salaries and pensions were severely cut and even the Commissars were paid only the same wage as a skilled worker.

Unlike the Tsars, Lenin and his colleagues refused to live in luxury while people starved (one important Bolshevik went around with holes in his boots). 'Loans' were demanded from the rich and one group of wealthy men in Kharkov were offered the choice of working in the coal mines or paying a Christmas bonus of one million roubles to their workers. Other changes were made in the alphabet, the calendar (altered to the western version, so that now the 'October' revolution is celebrated in November), marriage and divorce laws (divorce was made easier), and religion (churches could not own buildings etc. and religion could not be taught in schools.) Women were given equality with men and the old judges were replaced by new ones. A new, secret police, the Cheka, was formed to deal with the Bolsheviks' enemies. The idea was that

'The foe had to be made to feel that there was an all-seeing eye and a heavy punishing hand that would mercilessly fall on his head as soon as he made an attempt against Soviet power.

'All those against the revolution, all spies, ruffians, hooligans etc. will be mercilessly shot by the Cheka on the spot of the offence.'

In the summer of 1918 the 'Red Terror' began, following massacres of Bolshevik prisoners by Whites, the assassination of important Bolsheviks and an attempt to kill Lenin by the Socialist Revolutionaries. Large numbers of people were arrested and shot.

Meanwhile elections had been taking place for the 'Constituent Assembly', a body which was to be elected by every Russian and whose job was supposed to be the making of a *constitution*, a document which would say how Russia was to be governed. The elections had been arranged some time before the Bolshevik Revolution. Now the Bolsheviks knew how they thought Russia should be governed—by the Bolsheviks of course, and they were in no doubt as to what to do about the Constituent Assembly. The elections took place in mid-November and the Bolsheviks got about one quarter of the total vote. Most votes went to the Socialist Revolutionaries, the peasants' party. The Assembly met once only, on 5 January 1918, and found themselves surrounded by heavily armed Bolshevik soldiers who jeered and catcalled the various speakers. The Bolshevik members withdrew and once the Assembly had suspended its meeting it was prevented from meeting again by troops who barred the entrance to the meeting place. This attempt at *democratic* government had failed, partly because the Bolsheviks were obviously in control of the government, and partly because most Russians had no experience or understanding of democracy anyway.

The Bolsheviks then, were still in command and still faced by numerous problems. Of these, the greatest was peace. Lenin knew that the Bolsheviks must make peace if they were to remain in power. Therefore talks began with the Germans in a town called Brest-Litovsk. The Germans were astonished by the behaviour of some of the Russians at the talks—one had trouble using a knife and fork and another was mainly concerned to get as much strong drink as possible. However, an *armistice* was agreed—that is, fighting was to stop and peace talks, to settle the frontiers and other problems, were to follow.

In December 1917 some talks began, but they did not start properly till January. Trotsky was the main speaker for the Russians. The Germans soon proposed a new frontier which meant the loss of much land and many people by the Russians. Trotsky returned to Petrograd to talk the matter over with the other leading Bolsheviks. Some wished to continue fighting, but Lenin, Stalin and others realised that Russia could not continue to fight. To try to do so would make the Bolsheviks so unpopular that they would be unable to go on governing the country. 'Peace', after all, had been one of Lenin's main slogans. Trotsky's view was an odd one of 'no war and no peace'. And when he returned in February to Brest-Litovsk he showed what this meant. He refused to accept the German demands for Russian land, but said that the Russians would not fight and considered the war to be over. Trotsky was hoping that the German workers and soldiers would agree with him, overthrow their government, and stop fighting against

Trotsky and his colleagues met by German officers at Brest-Litovsk, January, 1918. Trotsky is at the extreme right

the Russians. However, the German generals merely ordered their troops to advance on Russia, and this they did. Lenin persuaded Trotsky that fighting must stop or the Bolshevik Revolution was doomed. 'We cannot joke with war.' So a message was sent to the Germans saying that the Russians were willing to make peace on the terms that the Germans had laid down in January. The Germans replied: the Bolsheviks could have peace, but on harsher and tougher terms which meant the loss of even more land. Lenin threatened to resign if peace was not made, and so, in March 1918, the treaty of Brest-Litovsk was signed (though not by Trotsky who refused to go).

FINLAND

Petrograd

● Moscow

Brest-Litovsk
●

U K R A I N E

--- Russian Boundary 1914

Line of Treaty of
Brest-Litovsk 1918

0   500

miles

The treaty was terribly severe. Russia lost Poland, the Baltic States, the Ukraine, and other lands in the west and south, amounting to one-quarter of her land and one-third of her people. Among the lost land were her richest farming areas (including the 'bread-basket' of the Ukraine) and most of her best factories and mines. Lenin argued, however, that the end of the war gave the Bolsheviks a 'breathing space' which would help them to strengthen their hold on Russia; and he was hopeful that the lost lands might be regained later. And, as so often happened, Lenin was right.

A Czech train on the Trans-Siberian Railway, June, 1918

12 Civil War

Peace had been made, but many Russians, especially those who had been officers in the Tsar's armies, thought it had been shameful because Russia had given up so much to Germany. These officers disliked the Bolshevik government anyway and many joined together in the south with Cossacks who hated the Bolsheviks. An army was growing there, when suddenly trouble appeared in another area altogether. There were some 45,000 Czechoslovakian prisoners-of-war in Russia who had been fighting for the Austrians against Russia, but who hated the Austrians and wanted to fight against them and their allies, the Germans. In the spring of 1918 they were travelling slowly along the Trans-Siberian railway towards Vladivostok, from where they were supposed to sail to France.

The Bolsheviks decided to send them out by the faster route through Murmansk, but the Czechs refused to accept this, and fought when the Bolsheviks tried to disarm them. Indeed, the Czechs gained control of a long stretch of the railway. Many people who hated the Bolsheviks began to fight against them, now that the Czechs were resisting too. So in the east the Soviet Government had some dangerous opponents who began to advance against Moscow. This was the moment where the local Bolshevik commander in Ekaterinburg had the Tsar and his family murdered in case they should fall into the hands of the Czechs and others. The Bolsheviks were afraid lest people might rally round the Tsar, though in fact almost no one wanted him restored to power.

Now Britain, France and the United States (the Allies) had been angered when the Bolsheviks withdrew Russia from the war, and had announced that all the loans that they had had would not be repaid. Moreover, there were huge dumps of arms and ammunition at Murmansk and Vladivostok, and the allies were afraid these might fall into German hands. So they decided to send troops to Russia. They hoped most of all to get the Russians to resume fighting against the Germans (who had been able to put most of their army on the Western Front) and thus make things easier for themselves. To get the Russians to resume the war meant to get rid of the people who had made peace—the Bolsheviks. Eventually, therefore, troops were sent to Vladivostok, Murmansk, and to various places in south Russia. In each place they helped the people who were fighting against the Bolsheviks. These opponents of the Bolsheviks were called 'Whites'.

The Bolsheviks were once more in grave danger. On all sides there were enemies—Russian 'Whites' supported by foreign armies, Czechs, British, French, American and Japanese. An army had to be created to resist these enemies,

Japanese troops marching through Vladivostok during the Allied Intervention

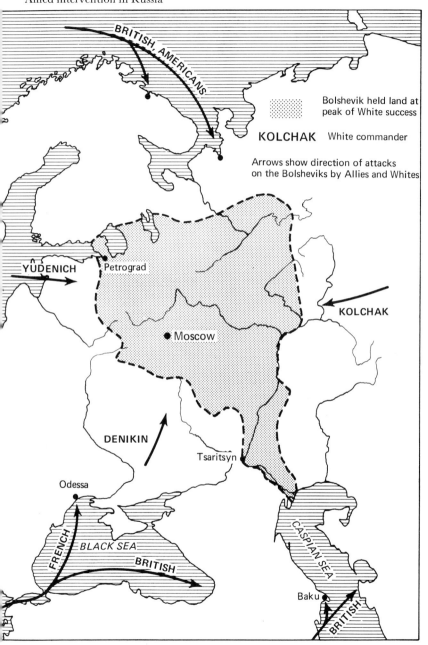

BRITISH, AMERICANS

Bolshevik held land at
peak of White success

KOLCHAK White commander

Arrows show direction of attacks
on the Bolsheviks by Allies and Whites

YŪDENICH

Petrograd

KOLCHAK

Moscow

DENIKIN

Tsaritsyn

Odessa

FRENCH

BLACK SEA

BRITISH

CASPIAN SEA

Baku

BRITISH

and Trotsky, did, in fact, create such an army in 1918. Trotsky directed the Bolshevik armies from a famous armoured train (the soldiers in which were all dressed in black leather with red stars in their peaked caps). He described his methods.

'Out of bands of *irregulars*, of refugees escaping from the Whites, of peasants, of workers we formed an army. Even after defeats the flabby, panicky mob could be changed into a useful force. What was needed for this? Good commanders, a few dozen experienced fighters, a dozen or so of Communists ready to make any sacrifice; boots for the barefooted, a bathhouse, food, underwear, tobacco. The train took care of all this . . . the shovelful of coal necessary at a particular moment to prevent the fire going out.'

Leon Trotsky as Commissar for War attending a Red Army parade in Red Square, Moscow

Lenin in October, 1919 encouraging troops setting off to fight the Whites

Officers were a problem, for the only ones with any experience were those who had fought for the Tsars, and the Bolsheviks did not trust them. What they did was to appoint commissars, Bolsheviks who kept a close watch on the officers to make sure that they were loyal to the Soviet Government. To provide enough troops for the new Red Army, the government introduced conscription, and the Cheka ensured that men joined up and did not desert. Units which showed cowardice in the battle were sometimes *decimated* afterwards—that is, every tenth man was taken out and shot.

The Red Army began a long battle against their 'White' opponents. By the end of 1918 four armies were pressing on the area held by the Bolsheviks.

Perhaps the most dangerous of these attacks was that from the east, led by Admiral Kolchak, who was assisted by the British. At one point his army reached the Volga, but he had no support from the peasants in Siberia and indeed some resisted him as *partisans*. Gradually he was pushed back and at length the Czechs handed him over to the Bolsheviks who shot him in early 1920. The Bolsheviks wrote a song about this:

The uniform is British,	The uniforms are tattered,
The *epaulettes* from France,	The epaulettes are gone,
Japan sends tobacco,	So is the tobacco, and
Kolchak leads the dance.	Kolchak's day is done.

The other White commanders also were eventually defeated by the Red Army, though only after terrible fighting and with great cruelty on both sides and terrible suffering for the Russian people. For example, in Siberia 'in one village on the Amur a number of people had taken refuge. Kolchak's governor encircled the place with White troops; a hole was made in the river and all the people driven under the ice.'

And, 'Everywhere the peasants were plundered, shot, hanged, thrashed and deprived of their lands.'

The worst offenders were the White commanders. Some, said a British newspaper man, showed bravery only 'in the restaurants of Vladivostok and Omsk, when late in the evening, they sometimes covered the members of the orchestra with their revolvers, and made them play "God save the Tsar". Many officers swindled their men of their food and drink.'

A British officer said of the White army of Kolchak: 'It was revolting to see wounded men dragging their way from station to hospital over dirty streets for perhaps a mile or two while officers rode scornfully by in *droshkies* or motor cars.' Some White officers were men of disgraceful character. One general in the south was thus described:

' . . . a terrible spectacle. His face was deadly pale and his mouth never ceased to tremble, while tears streamed from his eyes. . . . Incredible disorder reigned in his railway carriage. The table was covered with bottles and dishes of hors d'oeuvres; on the bunks were clothes, playing cards and weapons all lying about anyhow. Amidst all this confusion was Slachtov, clad in a fantastic white *dolman*, gold-laced and befurred. He was surrounded by all kinds of birds; he had a crane there, and also a raven, a swallow and a jay; they were hopping about on the table and the bunks, fluttering round and perching on their master's head and shoulders. . . . I insisted on General Slachtov undergoing a medical examination.'

The Bolsheviks won largely because the various White armies fought separately instead of together; because the White generals acted so foolishly and treated the people in their areas so harshly; and because after November 1918 (when the First World War came to an end) the main reason why the British and French had helped the Whites, that is, to keep Russia in the war, was gone. Gradually, the Allies withdrew their armies. The Bolsheviks had been in great peril, but once more they had won.

13 War Communism and the N.E.P.

While the civil war was raging, the ordinary Russian people were suffering terribly. Food was so short that *rationing* had to be introduced; people had to buy their food at a certain shop and were allowed only a limited amount (some black bread, a few herrings a month, and some sugar). If they were not working they got no ration cards and could not buy food in the shops. They had then to go to the 'Black Market'—usually stalls where people who had been rich took their furnishings and best clothes and exchanged them for food. The Moscow 'Black Market' was described by a writer like this:

> 'The Black Market sells everything. There the former rich are selling their last items. The best grand-piano sells for half the price of an ordinary record-player and both can be had for a trifle compared with the *astronomical* prices of food. The formerly richest and most spoiled are now satisfied if they get some black bread and potatoes each day. An acquaintance of mine, formerly owner of a palace in Moscow, was given, as his place of residence, the bath-room of his former home.'

Sometimes the Cheka raided the Black Market and took away stall owners and customers; sometimes stall holders who had hidden large amounts of food were shot.

Food was so short that many people became weakened and died of disease; it was hard to care for the sick because medicines were in short supply and doctors were few. The shops were mostly empty, tram-cars did not run, there was little wood or coal and people shivered through the Russian winter. A Bolshevik, Victor Serge, described what it was like to live in Russia at this time:

86

'Inside Petrograd's grand apartments people were crowded in one room, living around a little stove of brick or cast-iron which would be standing on the floor, its flue belching smoke through an opening in the window. Fuel for it would come from the floor boards nearby, from the last stick of furniture available, or else from books. Entire libraries disappeared in this way.'

Going to the theatre was the most popular entertainment, but the theatres were so cold that the audience had to huddle in their overcoats. The government, however, tried hard to care for the children because they were Russia's future citizens. The writer just quoted above went on to say:

'The Bolsheviks are making great efforts for the schools. The utmost is done for children from four to eight. These are taken care of in *kindergartens* where the teachers have them making figures in clay and the like. These children get the best of foods—*caviare*, sausage, butter—in sufficient quantities. They get good clothing and free shoes and laundry. They even provide the kindergartens with fine *porcelain* and beautiful linens and carpets from the mansions of the rich. The linens, napkins and the like are

Free dinners being served to Petrograd children, 1918

replaced by the teachers with ordinary rags and sold on the Black Market. The children come to school with collars of *lice* around their necks. The scarcity of soap makes it impossible for the parents to wash the children or the children's clothes.'

Lenin and the Bolsheviks, called Communists after March 1918, were bewildered by the difficulties produced by the Civil War, the food shortages and the failure of factories to produce as much as they had in 1914. At first it was decided to control the factories and farms very strictly. Most of the factories were nationalised and inspectors were appointed to watch over the factory managers and ensure that they did the job properly. But this did not work well and it became necessary to appoint inspectors to watch over the inspectors! And when the government tried to make sure that factories got enough fuel and supplies, something was generally forgotten. More and more people were employed in offices trying to ensure that the factories worked properly; but they did not succeed, and it meant only that fewer people were available to produce goods. So the shortages got worse, not better.

Lenin tried to act harshly towards the peasants also. They refused to sell their grain since there was nothing to buy with their roubles—the town factories were making practically nothing. The government therefore decided to force the peasants to hand over their grain in order to feed the town workers. Soldiers were sent to the villages to search for hidden supplies; poor peasants who informed against those who were hiding grain were given half of any discovered; the 'guilty' peasants were imprisoned. But this harsh plan failed. Serge tells us that 'parties which were sent into the countryside to obtain grain by *requisition* might be driven away or even killed by the peasants with pitchforks. Savage peasants would slit open a commissar's belly, pack it with grain, and leave him by the roadside as a lesson to all.' Peasants simply sowed less grain next season since they knew any surplus they had would be taken away and so there became even less available at the next year's harvest.

Finally, with peasants and workers alike very angry with the Communists, there was a revolt of sailors at Kronstadt in March 1921. Kronstadt had long been loyal to the Bolsheviks and though the revolt was crushed by the government Lenin realised that it must change its policy—'War Communism' had not been a success.

The main problem was that the factories were not producing enough goods to sell to the peasants who, therefore, would not produce enough grain to feed the factory workers. Lenin therefore decided to stop forcing the peasants to hand over grain; instead, a tax was placed on the peasant, and he could keep any surplus he managed to make and sell it. So the peasants were encouraged to work harder and produce more. In the town, too, the government kept hold of only the most important industries—like steel and the railways. But many smaller factories were returned to their old owners (if they were alive or could be found). Traders were allowed to work again, to get supplies to the factories, goods to the villages, and food into the shops. Lenin's scheme was called the New Economic Policy or N.E.P. and these traders, called Nepmen, often became rich quite quickly.

For a while the N.E.P. did not seem to be working. The peasants were suspicious of the government and there was a dreadful famine in the winter of 1921–22 in which five million people died. A visitor to Russia at this time described one village in this way:

'The children are not playing; they are walking about slowly like old people. We hardly meet half a dozen pigs in the whole village. All have been eaten or sold.

'They showed me many empty houses. In some cases the owners went away with their families in the hope of getting work in Siberia. Other men have gone but have left their families in the village, hoping that their wages will supplement the scanty harvest. Some have sold their houses for fuel, and we see empty places where some unfortunate has "eaten his house" as the peasants say.'

Aid from foreign countries helped Russia to recover from the

A starving child at Samara during the famine, 1921

famine and slowly things began to improve. New railway engines were imported from Germany, enabling goods to be moved around more quickly, more goods were produced in the factories, and the harvests became better. However, many workers and peasants continued to resent the rule of the Communists, and many Communists began to dislike the New Economic Policy. They felt that the peasants would have to produce more grain, so that Russia could export some in order to pay for machinery for more and more factories. But before anything was done about this, Lenin, the greatest of the Communists, had died.

14 Death of a Hero

Lenin leaving a meeting in 1918, followed by a woman, probably Dora Kaplan who shot him three times and severely wounded him

In 1918 a Socialist Revolutionary had made an attempt to assassinate Lenin. The attempt was unsuccessful, but Lenin was wounded in the neck, and the wound weakened him. He had a very severe illness in the spring of 1922 which left him partly *paralysed*, and though he recovered somewhat, he had another more severe attack of the same illness in the following year. Thereafter he lay in bed, unable to speak or write, until his death in January 1924. He was fifty-three years old. The city of Petrograd, the cradle of the Revolution, was re-named Leningrad in his honour. His body was taken from Gorki to Moscow, and the thirty-mile route was lined with people. 91

Lenin in his coffin, Gorki, 1924

Hundreds of thousands filed past the body as it *lay in state* in Moscow. The funeral was attended by all the great Bolsheviks —with one striking exception. Thereafter, Lenin's body was not buried or cremated; instead it was *embalmed* and placed in a specially built *mausoleum* in Red Square, Moscow (and is visited every year by millions of visitors to the city from Russia and all over the world). This was a sign that the Bolsheviks recognised that Lenin was a man of immense, almost super-human achievement.

What had he done? He had created the Bolshevik party which continues to rule Russia over forty years after his death. He had been the man who had convinced his party in 1917 that they could seize control of Russia, and he had been the brains behind the October Revolution which had proved he was right. He realized why the Provisional Government had been mistaken—in not giving the land to the peasants, in not trying to make peace, and he had allowed the peasants to keep the land and had made peace, even though it had been very unpopular. This made it possible for the Bolsheviks to win the Civil War against the Whites and their foreign helpers, and in the process Russia regained much of the land lost at Brest-Litovsk.

He had managed to do all this because he was a man of tremendous will power; because he knew more about organis-ing revolutions than anyone else; because he could out-argue his colleagues; and because he was completely sure that his own ideas were the right ones. He knew what kind of Russia he wanted—a Communist one, and he knew also that he would have to be ruthless to make it that way. Many thousands of people would have to be killed, and he accepted this (though he was not a cruel man); terror would have to be used (and he used the Cheka to hunt down his opponents); lies would have to be told. He once wrote: 'A Communist must be prepared to make every sacrifice and if necessary even resort to all sorts of schemes, use illegal methods, conceal the truth, in order to get into trade unions, stay there, and conduct revolutionary work within.'

He believed in Marx's idea of a class war. Lenin said: 'And what is this class struggle? It is the overthrow of the Tsar and the capitalists, and the destruction of the capitalist class.' Unlike Marx, however, he believed firmly that the revolution must be led by a party, the Bolsheviks, who would 'lead, organise, direct and fight for the people', and once the revolution had taken place, the party became the government of Russia, looking after the people, deciding what should be done for them.

Yet Lenin was a modest man who hated the fuss people made of him. He arranged to arrive late at a great celebration arranged in Moscow on his fiftieth birthday (he came at all so as not to offend the audience) and said, 'Thank you for two things: for today's greetings and even more for excusing me from listening to the speeches.' He objected to the way in which the Bolshevik newspapers praised him and it is certain that he would not have approved of the Lenin Mausoleum (as his wife Krupskaya did not).

It was a great tragedy for Russia that he died so young, for his reputation was so great that it is almost certain that he could have ruled Russia better than the man who succeeded him. And many terrible events which occurred between 1924 and 1941 might never have happened.

When it became clear in 1922 that Lenin would probably never recover, the Bolsheviks began to consider who would succeed him as leader of the party, and hence of Russia. There were three main candidates, and a struggle soon developed among them. One was Zinoviev, a good speaker and able writer. He had returned with Lenin in 1917, but had opposed him over the October Revolution. His main difficulty was that he was not very effective when things were going badly. As Trotsky put it, 'When things took a bad turn Zinoviev usually stretched himself on a sofa and sighed.' Trotsky himself was the second main possibility. He was the next most famous Bolshevik after Lenin and had shared with him the task of carrying out the October Revolution. Yet he and Lenin had often quarrelled, especially over the peace of Brest-Litovsk, and many Bolsheviks resented the fact that Trotsky had not joined the party until the summer of 1917. Trotsky was clumsy in his dealings with people, took offence easily, and was unpleasant to those who disagreed with him. His greatest achievement had been his work as Commissar for War and his fellow Commissar (for Education) Lunacharsky wrote that, though Lenin was a greater thinker than Trotsky, Lenin could 'never have coped with the titanic mission which Trotsky took on his own shoulders, with those lightning moves from place to place, those astounding speeches, those on-the-spot orders, being the electrifier of a weakening army, now at one spot, now at another'.

Trotsky himself was fairly certain that Lenin meant him to be his successor so that he made little effort to ensure it.

The third candidate was Joseph Stalin. He said little, and many thought him unimportant, but gradually he made himself very powerful in the Bolshevik party, especially after he became General Secretary in April 1922. This meant that he could appoint a large number of the party officials, and he appointed people loyal to himself. By the end of 1922 Lenin had realised that Stalin was brutal and harsh, and in a famous will advised his colleagues that 'Stalin is too rough, and this the General Secretary should not be. Thus I suggest that the comrades think of some means of displacing Stalin and putting in his place someone more civil and considerate . . .'

Towards the end Lenin's support went to Trotsky, but he

Carrying Lenin's body. Stalin is second from the right

did little or nothing to try to deal with Stalin. Anyway Stalin had formed a temporary friendship with Zinoviev to defeat Trotsky. When Lenin died Trotsky was on holiday, recovering from an illness. Stalin took over control immediately, assisted by Zinoviev, and Trotsky did not even attend Lenin's funeral (he said that Stalin had told him the wrong date).

Stalin then became ruler of Russia. Soon he became a dictator like the Tsar, only far more ruthless. His secret police were far more thorough than the Okhrana ever were. People were sent into exile, but few ever escaped. Trotsky was expelled, first from the party, then from Russia. Even then Stalin was not satisfied and in 1940 Trotsky was assassinated in Mexico City by one of Stalin's agents. Zinoviev was shot in 1936 at a time when Stalin was brutally executing anyone he suspected of being in opposition to him. Stalin's rule was harsh, but he made Russia a great industrial country, the equal of the United States. But the real creator of modern Russia, the first Communist state in the history of the world, was Vladimir Ilyich Ulyanov—Lenin.

Note on Dates

Until the spring of 1918 Russia used a different calendar from that of Western Europe. The Russian *Julian* calendar was thirteen days behind the Western *Gregorian* calendar in the twentieth century, so that the date 18 April 1917 in London would in Petrograd be given as 5 April 1917. The two revolutions of 1917 happened near the end of the month by the Julian calendar, so that the February and October revolutions (as the Russians reckoned them) happened in March and November by the Western reckoning. This is why the Russians now celebrate the Bolshevik 'October' Revolution in November. The dates given in this book are in the Julian Calendar until the spring of 1918 when it ceased to be used.

Things to Do

1. Make a scrap-book about the Soviet Union. Include any pictures you can find, especially ones of the different nationalities. Show by maps where the different peoples live, and find out about their languages and customs.
2. Make a time chart for the year 1917. Use frieze-paper and put the months along the top. For each important event make a short written summary and draw or paint a picture of the events.
3. Many plays have been written about the Bolshevik Revolution. Try to write short scenes about:
   (a) The meeting of the Central Committee where Lenin persuaded the Bolsheviks to carry out the Revolution.
   (b) The Bolshevik argument over the Treaty of Brest-Litovsk.
   (c) A discussion among the Bolsheviks about the setting up of the Cheka.
4. Write a newspaper report on the abdication of the Tsar.
5. Write some extracts from a diary of a Russian soldier: going off to war; fighting the Germans; helping the wounded; deserting.
6. Imagine you took part in the storming of the Winter Palace. Describe the events of the night.
7. Several Russian cities in addition to Petrograd have changed their names since 1917. Find out as many of these as you can and try to discover after whom they were named.
8. Write an *obituary* of Lenin.
9. Find out who has ruled Russia from Lenin's death till the present.
10. Find out what the 'Zinoviev' letter was about.
11. Find out about Makhno, Deniken, Wrangel, Kolchak.
12. Many pictures have been painted about the events of the Revolution and Civil War. Choose an event or scene which interests you and paint a picture of it.

How Do We Know?

Often, when people study the past to find out what happened, they find it difficult because there is too little information. This is not so in the case of the Russian Revolution. Far more has been written about it than anyone could ever hope to read in a lifetime; this is a sign of how important an event people think it is. So one problem is that there is too much material. But there is another problem also: many of the people involved in the Revolution wrote accounts of what happened, but their accounts are *biased*, that is they try to show that they were wise and right, and their enemies were foolish and wrong and evil. This is true of Alexander Kerensky's account, for example. And in Russia while Stalin was ruling and even today, Trotsky's part in the Revolution has been ignored or falsified, and the part played by Stalin made more important than it had been. So every account has to be weighed against other accounts to try to find out the truth.

The *sources* of our knowledge include eye-witness accounts (like John Reed's 'Ten Days that Shook the World' and Konstantin Paustovsky's 'Story of a Life'), letters (especially those from the Tsar to the Tsaritsa), accounts by people who took part in the Revolution ('The Kerensky Memoirs') or who worked for foreign governments (Bruce Lockart's 'Memoirs of a British Agent'). Other information comes from the writings of people like Lenin, from accounts of Lenin, Trotsky and others written at the time (especially those by the Bolshevik Lunacharsky) and from interviews made later (Prince Yusupov was interviewed by a reporter from the English newspaper, the 'Guardian', on the fiftieth anniversary of Rasputin's assassination).

Newspaper reports are helpful also, and many photographs are available to show what particular people or places looked like. And many of the places connected with the Revolution—such as the Winter Palace, the Kremlin—still survive and can be visited. In Russia there are museums which are concerned with preserving

information and objects connected with the Revolution. However, scholars from outside Russia cannot see many of the papers they would like to because the Soviet Government forbids this (as many governments do). Some official papers are available, however, and can be used. Out of all of these papers and accounts we can find out much about the Revolution.

An example of an historical document: the Bolshevik Proclamation of 25 October, 1917, announcing their seizure of power

Further Reading

Jackdaw No. 42: 'The Russian Revolution' (Cape)
John Reed: 'Ten Days that Shook the World' (Penguin)
E. M. Roberts: 'Lenin and the Downfall of Tsarist Russia' (Methuen)
John Fisher: 'The True Book about the Russian Revolution' (Muller)
Sally Pickering: '20th Century Russia' (Oxford University Press)
Louis Snyder: 'The First Book of the Soviet Union' (Ward)
John Robottom: 'Modern Russia' (Longmans)

Glossary

to abdicate, to give up the throne

Ambassador, man sent to another country to represent his own country there

Archduke, the heir to the Austrian throne

armistice, halt in the fighting to allow peace talks to take place

arsenal, place for storing weapons and ammunition

to assassinate, to murder, usually some important person

astronomical, here means very high (as high as the stars)

autocrat, ruler who does not share his power with anyone else

battalions, large groups of soldiers (usually about 1,000 or so)

bias, to slant an account in one's own favour

Black Earth, belt of rich soil that stretches from the Ukraine into Siberia

blockade, shutting-off of a place to prevent supplies reaching an enemy

Bolsheviks, revolutionaries who followed the ideas of Karl Marx and believed that the Tsar's government should be overthrown by a violent revolution

cadets, men being trained as officers

capitalists, those who owned the mines, factories, banks etc.

Caucasian, from the Caucasus, in south Russia—between the Black Sea and the Caspian

cauldrons, huge saucepans

caviare, delicacy to eat, made from the roe of a fish—sturgeon

census, a count of all the people of a country to find out the ages, family size, work etc. for the government's records.

Cheka, secret police set up by the Bolsheviks in 1918 once they had become the rulers of Russia

classes, large groups of people in a country who are divided by incomes, kind of work etc.

co-author, had worked with another in the writing of a book

code, method of disguising signals or messages

to commandeer, to seize for use by the army or government

communism, to Marx it meant that the people of a country would own its factories, banks etc. Marx thought that this would happen only after a revolution

Communist Manifesto, book written by Marx and Engels in 1848 which set out some of the aims of Communism

conscripts, soldiers compelled to serve in the army

constitution, arrangement made for governing Russia

co-operatives, groups of farmers who agreed to work and sell their produce together, each helping the others

Cossacks, men from South Russia who acted as cavalry for the Tsar

Das Kapital, book in which Marx and Engels explained fully the aims of communism

decimated, every tenth man shot

decrees, regulations

delegate, someone chosen by a group of men to speak for them at a meeting

democratic, the people have the right of free choice

discipline, obedience to rules

dispersal, scattering, breaking up

dolman, long cloak with wide sleeves

droshky, two- or four-wheeled cart

Duma, group elected by some of the Russian people to give advice to the Tsar

dynasty, ruling family

Eastern Front, area where the Russians fought the German and Austrians

embalmed, preserved with spices and drugs

epaulettes, badges of rank worn on the shoulder

exile, living far from home or country, usually as a punishment

freight, goods, luggage

garrison, troops permanently stationed in a town to protect it or keep order

God save the Tsar, Russian national anthem before the Revolution

Gregorian calendar, western calendar which we still use

Greek Orthodox Church, State Church of Russia before the Revolution

haemophilia, physical disability which leads to bleeding on the slightest bump; the bleeding is very hard to stop

independence, freedom to run their own affairs

infantry, soldiers who fight on foot

intercepted, stopped and examined before being delivered

irregulars, fighters who were not part of any regular recognised force

Julian calendar, used in Russia till spring 1918; 13 days behind the Gregorian

junkers, officers-to-be in training

kindergartens, nursery schools for very young children

knout, many-thonged whip formerly used in Russia for beating prisoners

kopeks, Russian coins of little value

Kremlin, Russian word for fortress, used mainly for the building in Moscow which houses many government departments

kulaks, wealthy peasants

labour camps, camps where prisoners were sent to work during their sentence

last rites, blessing given to the dying

to lie in state, to lie displayed for viewing before the funeral

lice, plural of louse—small insect which infests people's hair or bodies and can spread disease

lynched, put to death without judgment by law

mausoleum, magnificent tomb

Menshevik, member of a minority party of the Revolution

mobilisation, getting armies ready for battle and sending them off to the front

nationalised, the property taken over by the State

New Economic Policy, effort made to make Bolshevik Government more popular and effective by allowing some private trade and enabling peasants to keep a portion of their produce

obituary, account of a person published at the time of his death

oblivious, unaware of

occupation, kind of work done

Okhrana, Tsar's secret police

ovation, enthusiastic welcome

paralysed, unable to use his limbs

partisans, irregular soldiers fighting behind the enemies lines

porcelain, fine china

Pravda, the Bolshevik newspaper (the word 'pravda' means 'truth')

to predict, to foretell the future

proclamations, statements telling out a party's aims—generally briefly and strongly

to procure, to get hold of

proletariat, wage-earning workers

propaganda, persuading people to support some idea or party

provisional, temporary

rationing, limiting the amount of food (or any other supply) each person gets

registration, putting people's names on a list or register

reinforcements, additional troops

requisition, taking for the Government's use, often without payment

revered, loved

103

revolution, violent overthrow of a government

roubles, Russian money

Russification, effort to make non-Russian people adopt Russian customs and language

samovar, kind of kettle for making tea

Serbian, citizen of Serbia, a small country which now forms part of Yugoslavia

serfs, peasants who were forced to work for a particular landowner who could sell them if he wished

slogans, phrases which sum up in a few words the aims of a group of people or party

sniping, firing at people from a concealed position

Social Democrat, Russian group who followed the ideas of Karl Marx

socialism, the idea that factories, the land etc. of a country should belong to the people

Socialist Order, communist state as the Bolsheviks wanted it

Socialist Revolutionaries, party which believed that the peasants were the main strength of Russia

source, book, building, thing, from which we can get information

Soviet, council—usually of workers, soldiers and peasants

street-car, tramcar running on tracks laid in the street and going on electric power from overhead wires

treaties, agreements signed between one country and another

Tsar, Emperor of Russia

Tsaritsa, Empress

ultimatum, final offer of terms before taking action to enforce acceptance

vaulted, with an arched ceiling

volley, firing by a group of soldiers at one time

Western Front, area where the French and British fought the Germans

Zemstvos, councils set up to govern the country areas of Russia; the members were elected by the wealthier people

Zeppelins, German airships

zero hour, hour when the attack begins